TOP **10**
CORFU
& THE IONIANS

CAROLE FRENCH

DK

EYEWITNESS TRAVEL

035

D0185111

Left **Lefkáda marina** Right **Blue Caves, Zákynthos**

DK

LONDON, NEW YORK,
MELBOURNE, MUNICH AND DELHI
www.dk.com

Reproduced by Colourscan, Singapore
Printed and bound in China by
Leo Paper Products Ltd.

First published in Great Britain in 2010
by Dorling Kindersley Limited
80 Strand, London WC2R 0RL
A Penguin Company

A CIP catalogue record is available from the
British Library.

ISBN 978 1 4053 4818 8

Within each Top 10 list in this book, no
hierarchy of quality or popularity is implied.
All 10 are, in the editor's opinion, of roughly
equal merit.

Contents

Corfu & the Ionians' Top 10

Left **Divarata village, Kefalloniá** Right **The Monastery of the Virgin of Vlacherna, Corfu**

Left **Limestone cliffs, Mýrtou Bay, Kefalloniá** Right **Venetian-style architecture, Zákynthos Town**

Opening times for sights in this book are usually given for "summer" (Easter–Oct) and "winter" (Nov–Easter); call ahead to confirm.

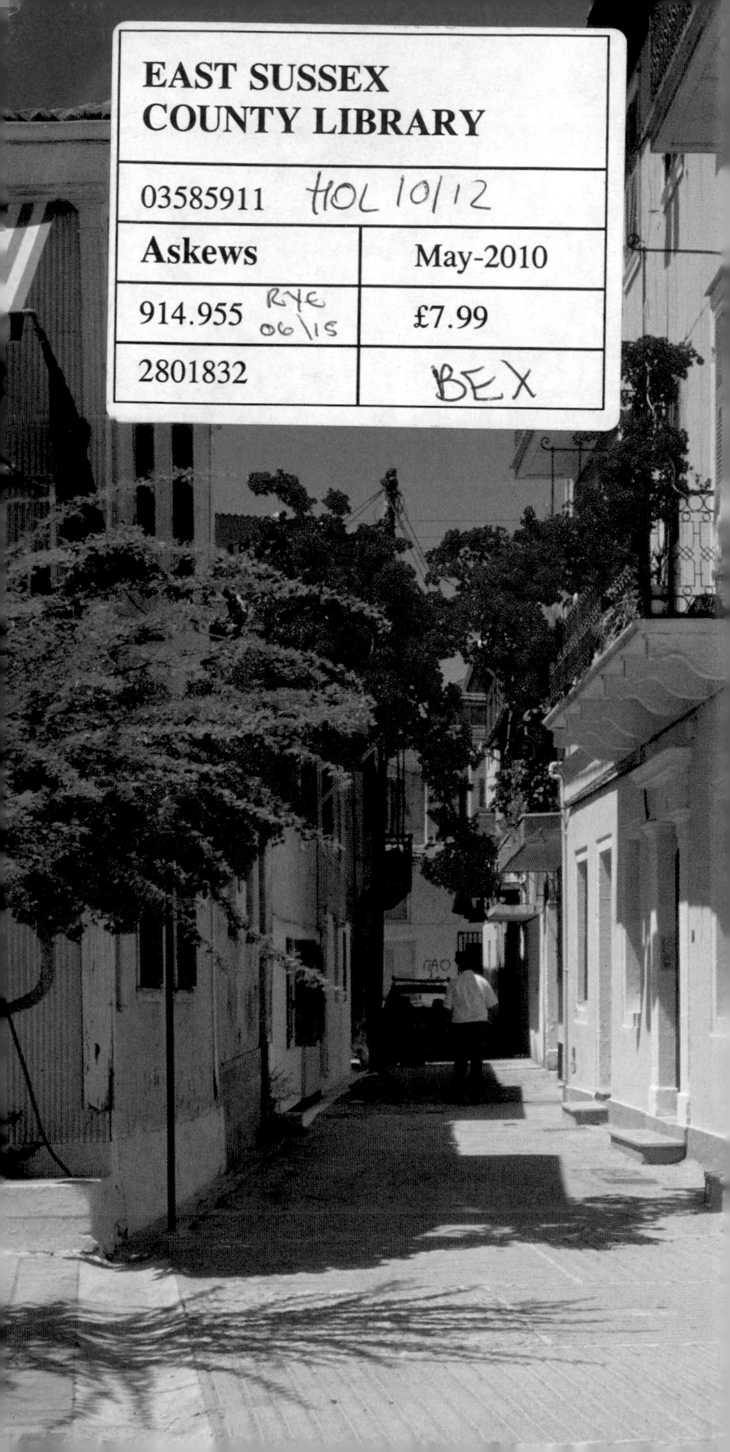

CORFU &
THE IONIANS'
TOP 10

Corfu and the Ionians' Highlights

The widely scattered Ionian islands, which lie off the western coast of mainland Greece, include Corfu (Kerkyra in Greek), Paxí, Antipaxí, Lefkáda, Kefaloniá, Ithaki and Zákynthos. They are the most verdant of all the Greek islands and offer a fabulous array of attractions. Olive groves, lush forests and sleepy, rural villages lie inland, while along the coasts are year-round holiday resorts and stunning beaches. Ancient sights, including the "living museum" of the UNESCO-listed Corfu Old Town, attract history enthusiasts, and the agreeable climate makes the islands popular with sailors

• Sidári
Barbati
Pyrgí
Paleokastrítsa
CORFU TOWN
see map right
Corfu
Benítses
Moraitika
Lefí

1 Corfu Old Town
The oldest part of Corfu Town is a delightful blend of architectural styles. It boasts imposing fortresses, which once offered protection, the French-style Liston, with its arcaded terraces, the tranquil Plateia Spianáda and the elegant Palace of St Michael and St George.

2 Archaeological Museum, Corfu Town
This museum has one of the country's finest collections of ancient artifacts. It includes the stunning Gorgon Medusa pediment from the Temple of Artemis, one of the oldest pediments in the Mediterranean *(see pp10–11)*.

3 Mon Repos Estate, Corfu
Built by Sir Frederick Adam, the second British Lord High Commissioner of the Ionians, Mon Repos later became the summer home of the Greek royals. Within its grounds lie major archaeological finds *(see pp12–13)*.

4 Achílleion Palace, Corfu
A popular attraction with visitors, the Achílleion Palace was built for the Empress Elisabeth of Austria in the 1890s and later became the home of Germany's Kaiser Wilhelm II. Marvel at the collection of paintings and personal belongings of the palace's former owners *(see pp14–15)*.

5 Mýrtou Bay Area, Kefaloniá
Described as one of the most beautiful beaches in the world, Mýrtou Bay is well known for its exquisite turquoise sea, dazzling white beach and lush surroundings. Located nearby are the picturesque villages of Divarata and Agia Effimia *(see pp16–17)*.

Preceding pages **A narrow alleyway, Lefkáda Town**

Caves of Sámi, Kefalloniá 6

The impressive caves of Sámi include the enormous Drogkaráti cave, with its stalactites and stalagmites, and the underground Melissáni cave and lake *(see pp18–19)*.

Zákynthos Town 7

The capital of Zákynthos, this town boasts Venetian-style architecture, with Neo-Classical buildings and large squares. After the devastating earthquake of 1953, Zákynthos Town was rebuilt in its original style *(see pp20–21)*.

Byzantine Museum, Zákynthos Town 8

This popular museum houses a breathtaking collection of Byzantine ecclesiastical art and icons. It also includes a scale model of Zákynthos Town, showing how the island's capital looked before the 1953 earthquake *(see pp22–3)*.

Lefkáda Town 9

Lefkáda Town is known for its unusual architecture of timber-framed buildings clad with colourful sheets of metal. This charming town has narrow streets, atmospheric tavernas, unique museums and a busy harbour *(see pp24–5)*.

Sailing Around the Ionians 10

With a good choice of marinas and anchorages and a mild climate, the islands are popular sailing destinations. The sea here can be explored privately or on organized cruises *(see pp26–7)*.

The Ionian islands are also collectively called the Heptanese, or "the seven islands".

🔟 Corfu Old Town

With its cobbled plazas and tiny alleyways dating back to Roman times, Corfu Old Town continues to retain its old-world charm. Palaces, museums, fortresses, gourmet restaurants, traditional tavernas, cultural venues and a lively harbour combine to give the town its inimitable character. It has beautiful arcades reminiscent of the finest in Paris along with elegant Venetian mansions, which line the town's main thoroughfare, the Kapodistrou. Add Greek, Italian and British influences and you have an eclectic architectural anthology.

Cafés lining the arched Liston, Corfu Old Town

🔵 Enjoy a cup of coffee and a pastry at one of the Liston's cafés.

• Palaio Frourio: Map Q1; Palaio Frourio Islet; 26610 48310; open summer: 8am–7:30pm daily; winter: 8am–3pm daily; adm €4
• Neo Frourio: Map P1; Plateia Solomóu; 26610 27370; open May–Nov: 9am–8pm daily; adm €3
• Church of St Spyrídon: Map P5; Ag Spyridonos; 2661033059; open 10am–1pm daily
• Palace of St Michael and St George and Museum of Asiatic Art: Map Q5; Plateia Spianáda; 26610 30443; open summer: 8:30am–8pm Tue–Sun, 1:30–8pm Mon; winter: 8:30am–3pm Tue–Sun; adm €3
• Antivouniotissa Museum: Map P4; Prosforou 30; 26610 38313; open summer: 8am–7:30pm daily; winter: 8:30am–3pm Tue–Sun; adm €2 adults, €1 concessions

Top 10 Features

1. Palaio Frourio
2. Neo Frourio
3. Plateia Spianáda
4. The Liston
5. Maitland Monument
6. Church of St Spyrídon
7. Palace of St Michael and St George
8. Dimarchio
9. The Old Port
10. Antivouniotissa Museum

1 Palaio Frourio

Palaio Frourio (Old Fortress) stands on an islet separated from the mainland by a moat. This 16th-century fort boasts beautiful interiors and hosts cultural events all year. St George's Church, noted for its Doric columns, stands at its base.

2 Neo Frourio

The Venetians built this mighty fort *(left)* in the 1500s to strengthen the town's defences. Despite its name, Neo Frourio (New Fortress) was completed only a few years after the Old Fortress. The Greek navy occupied it for many years and now it is open to the public.

3 Plateia Spianáda

A haven for anyone who likes to read, run or simply take refuge from the summer heat under the trees or the bandstand *(right)*, this is the town's largest square. It is divided in two by Viktoros Dousmani Street to create Ano Plateia and Kato Plateia.

➡ *Corfu Old Town was designated a UNESCO World Heritage Site in 2007.*

The Liston

An iconic Old Town sight, the Liston was built in 1807 by Mathieu de Lesseps, a Frenchman. Known for its arcaded terraces and stylish cafés, this is a fine example of the architecture of the Napoleonic period. The terrace was inspired by the Rue de Rivoli in Paris.

Maitland Monument

Dominating Plateia Spianáda, this 19th-century monument *(above)* is reminiscent of a Roman rotunda. It was built to commemorate the life of Sir Thomas Maitland, the first Lord High Commissioner of the Ionians (1815–23) during the British administration.

Church of St Spyrídon

Named after Corfu's patron saint, St Spyrídon, whose remains lie here in a lavish silver coffin, this 16th-century church is an Old Town landmark. It has a distinct red-topped campanile with bells that ring out at regular intervals.

Palace of St Michael and St George

This Georgian-style building, which was once home to the Greek royal family, has been at the forefront of local history for decades. The palace also houses the fabulous Museum of Asiatic Art.

Dimarchio

The Dimarchio, or Town Hall, is a classic Venetian-style building that was once the San Giacomo theatre, a favourite haunt of the island's nobility.

Antivouniotissa Museum

Housed in the Church of Panagia (Our Lady) Antivouniotissa, this charming museum *(above)* contains a superb collection of Byzantine and post-Byzantine icons and exquisite ecclesiastical treasures.

The Old Port

Once an integral part of Corfu Town's fortifications, the ancient Old Port *(below)* is one of the prettiest places in the area. It is a popular place to anchor cruise ships, although nowadays many head for the more modern New Port, a little distance to the east.

The Mános Collection

The focus of Corfu Old Town's Museum of Asiatic Art, the Mános Collection comprises around 11,000 impressive pieces of Chinese, Japanese and Korean furnishings, ceramics and weapons, plus some miniature works of art. Corfiot diplomat Grigórios Mános (1850–1929) amassed the fascinating collection during his travels and was instrumental in establishing the museum. Mános was alive to see it open in 1927, but he died several months later.

For more on the Museum of Asiatic Art **See p39.**

TOP 10 Archaeological Museum, Corfu Town

Located near the seafront, a short walk from Corfu Old Town, the Archaeological Museum has become one of the most notable institutions in Greece. It was originally founded in the 1960s to display finds from the ancient Temple of Artemis, including the impressive Gorgon Medusa pediment. Two further exhibition halls were added in the 1990s to house priceless acquisitions unearthed during excavation work at and around the citadel site at Kassiópi (see p60), on the north coast of Corfu.

Archaeological Museum, Corfu Town

⚙️ Ask for a special ticket if you are also planning to go to the Antivouniotissa Museum and the Palaio Frourio *(see pp8–9)* – for around €10 you can visit all three sights.

🥤 The seafront walk from Corfu Old Town to the museum is dotted with cafés serving refreshing, cool drinks.

• Map P2
• Vraila Armeni Street, Corfu Town
• 26610 30680
• Open 8:30am–3pm Tue–Sun
• Adm €3
• www.odysseus. culture.gr

Top 10 Features

1. Temple of Artemis Collection
2. Gorgon Medusa Pediment
3. Ancient Citadel Collection
4. Artifacts from Kassiópi
5. Lion of Menecrates Sculpture
6. Running Young Reveller Bronze
7. Marble Apollo
8. Dionýsus Pediment
9. Ancient Coin Collection
10. Hoplite Armour Collection

1 Temple of Artemis Collection

This collection includes 5th-century-BC terracotta statues of Artemis, the Hellenic goddess of forests and hunting, as well as household items and coins unearthed from the original temple at Kanóni.

3 Ancient Citadel Collection

Excavations around Corfu Town have unearthed busts and figurines, including one of a young woman, whose features are almost intact. This unique collection, with its vases, friezes and vessels, some of which are painted, gives fascinating insights into ancient Greek lifestyles.

2 Gorgon Medusa Pediment

Originally part of the Temple of Artemis, a Hellenic seat of worship, the Gordon Medusa pediment *(above)* is a 17-m-(56-ft-) long frieze depicting the snake-haired Medusa and her children. The pediment dates from around 590 BC and is the most important exhibit in the museum.

4 Artifacts from Kassiópi

A section of the museum is dedicated to the finds unearthed during excavation work in Kassiópi village, the site of a 13th-century fortress. Exhibits include well-preserved ceramics and coins. Ruins of the fortress can be visited *(see p60)*.

The Temple of Artemis was located at Kanóni on the outskirts of Corfu Town, on the present-day Mon Repos Estate (see pp12–13).

5 Lion of Menecrates Sculpture
Dating from the 7th century BC, this famous sculpture of a crouching lion *(right)* was discovered near the tomb of the sculptor Menecrates, in present-day Corfu Town, on Alkinou Street, and is now housed in the museum's upper floor. A funerary artifact, this sculpture is beautifully crafted in the Corinthian style of the Archaic period.

6 Running Young Reveller Bronze
The skilfully crafted bronze statue of a *commastes* (a young reveller), shown with a *rhyton* (a libation vessel) in his hand, is an exhibit here. Although its origins are unclear, the bronze bears the features of the workmanship of ancient Sparta's Laconian region.

7 Marble Apollo
Dating from around AD 150, the subtly lit marble Apollo statue *(below)*, although only a torso, is an imposing sight in the main entrance hall. It is a copy of the Parnopias Apollo statue by Pheidias, a 5th-century-BC sculptor.

8 Dionýsus Pediment
Depicting a meeting of ancient Greek officials who are surrounded by their animals and possessions, this beautifully carved pediment *(main image)* is a good example of 5th-century-BC workmanship. It was discovered in the Figareto area outside Corfu Town.

9 Ancient Coin Collection
The museum's ancient coin collection *(left)* has been amassed through excavations around the island, and spans many periods. Interestingly, it includes foreign, as well as Greek coins, suggesting that trade with other countries was prolific in Greece in ancient times. The collection is one of the finest in Greece.

10 Hoplite Armour Collection
A selection of interesting items, including helmets and breast plates, form this collection *(right)*. These protective garments were once worn by the Hoplites, a band of soldiers famous for their use of round shields. They were the protectors of the city kingdoms in ancient times.

Medusa
With snakes for hair and haunting eyes, Medusa, a gorgon, has had her place in legend for centuries and is one of the most well-known Greek mythological figures. It is said that anyone who looked at her would be turned to stone. The Gorgon Medusa pediment, from the west façade of the Temple of Artemis, shows her with her children – Chrysaor, the warrior, and Pegasus, the flying horse.

For more information on museums **See pp38–9.**

Mon Repos Estate, Corfu

With its seemingly endless lush gardens set atop the hill of Analipsis at Kanóni, the Mon Repos Estate is a haven of tranquillity. It was created during British rule by the second Lord High Commissioner of the Ionians, Sir Frederick Adam. The estate later became the summer home of the Greek royal family, and, in turn, the birthplace of Prince Philip, the Duke of Edinburgh. It is also famous for being the site of Palaeopolis, the island's ancient city. It is possible to visit the remains of ancient buildings in the grounds, such as those of the 5th-century St Kerkyra Basilica.

Ruins of St Kerkyra Basilica, Mon Repos Estate

An information board just inside the main entrance points you in the right direction for the sights.

Although water is available, there are no refreshment stops in the Mon Repos Estate, so be sure to take some soft drinks with you.

• Map Q3
• Mon Repos Estate: Kanóni, Corfu Town; 26610 20980; open summer: 8:30am–8pm daily, winter: 8am–5pm daily; adm free; pets allowed in the grounds
• Mon Repos Palace and the Museum of Palaeopolis: 26610 41369; open Apr–Oct: 8:30am–8pm Tue–Sun, 1–8pm Mon; adm €3

Top 10 Features

1. Mon Repos Palace
2. Museum of Palaeopolis
3. Hellenistic Mosaic Collection
4. The Gardens
5. Ruins of the Temple of Apollo
6. Ruins of the Temple of Hera
7. Roman Baths
8. Hellenistic Agora
9. Ruins of St Kerkyra Basilica
10. Alkinoos Harbour

Mon Repos Palace
An elegant Neo-Classical building with attractive entrance columns and bay windows, the palace *(main image)* was built in 1824 as the home of the British Lord High Commissioner of the Ionians. The palace is open to visitors.

Museum of Palaeopolis
Housed within the palace, this superb museum displays ancient archaeological treasures, such as Doric columns, which sit surprisingly well alongside the refined clothing, household items and furniture from the time of British rule.

Hellenistic Mosaic Collection
The museum houses an impressive floor-mosaic collection discovered at the St Kerkyra Basilica in the Mon Repos grounds. Restored during the 1960s, the mosaics depict scenes featuring the gods of the Hellenistic period.

The Gardens
Laid over 100 ha (250 acres), the gardens *(left)* bring together lavish Mediterranean shrubs and flowers, lawns and trees with historical remains – look out for Doric columns, the remains of a harbour, an agora and Roman baths.

5 Ruins of the Temple of Apollo

The ruins of what is considered to have been a fabulous temple can be found in the grounds of the palace. Built in a Doric style complete with a row of pillars, it is believed to have been dedicated to the god Apollo, who was the son of Zeus and the brother of Artemis.

6 Ruins of the Temple of Hera

The remains of this Doric-style temple *(right)* lie near the palace. Dating back to the 4th century BC, it is said to have been ancient Corfu's largest temple. The stonework remains suggest that this was built using advanced architectural methods of the day.

7 Roman Baths

These Roman baths *(below)* include a heating chamber and an under-floor hypocaust for the circulation of hot air. The baths date back to around AD 200 and the reign of Emperor Septimus Severus.

8 Hellenistic Agora

The agora, discovered during excavations about 60 years ago, was at the heart of the island's commercial activity in ancient times. Here, traders used to stand on large stone slabs offering their wares.

9 Ruins of St Kerkyra Basilica

Dedicated to St Kerkyra, this basilica was an important church in the 5th century AD. It was built to resemble a crucifix from above, and its entrance porticos and the transept (the horizontal part of the crucifix shape) are still worth seeing.

10 Alkinoos Harbour

The remains of a harbour *(above)*, named after King Alkinoos, who featured in Homer's *The Odyssey*, were found at around the same time as an ancient dockyard. Nearby are remains of what are believed to have once been the homes of wealthy merchants.

Sir Frederick Adam

Sir Frederick Adam (1781–1853) became the second Lord High Commissioner of the Ionians in 1824 after a distinguished career in the British army – he commanded the 3rd Light Brigade during the Battle of Waterloo (1815). Mon Repos Estate was built as a gift for his wife, Nina, although the couple only lived in the palace for a few years before Sir Frederick was posted to the governorship of Madras, India, in 1932.

🔟 Achílleion Palace, Corfu

This Neo-Classical palace was built in the late 1890s for the Empress Elisabeth of Austria, best known as Princess Sissi. It was the work of Raphael Carita, a much-respected Italian architect of the day. The empress, who adored Corfu, is said to have used it as a retreat from her stressful life at the Habsburg court. Following her assassination by an anarchist in 1898, the palace remained empty until Germany's Kaiser Wilhelm II bought it in 1907. Today, it is one of Corfu's most popular sights.

The imposing façade of the Achilleion Palace

🚗 The palace lies in the village of Gastouri, a short distance south along the coast road from Corfu Town.

🍴 There are a few tavernas in the village and a kiosk near the entrance to the palace for soft drinks and snacks.

- Map D4
- Gastouri, outskirts of Corfu Town
- 26610 56210
- Open Apr–Oct: 8am–7pm daily; Nov–Mar: 8:30am–3pm daily
- Adm €7

Top 10 Features

1. The Main Hall
2. Four Seasons
3. Peristyle of the Muses Hall
4. Palace Collection of Paintings
5. Kaiser's Room
6. Empress Elisabeth's Catholic Chapel
7. Statues of Hera and Zeus
8. Statues of Goddesses in the Gardens
9. Statue of the Dying Achilles
10. Kaiser's Bridge

The Main Hall
The entrance hall *(main image)* to the palace is dominated by a massive marble staircase to the first floor and stunning ceiling decorations, the most notable of which is the *Four Seasons* fresco.

Four Seasons
Painted by Galoppi, a 19th-century Italian artist, the fabulous *Four Seasons* fresco is an impressive sight. The painting depicts female figures who represent the seasons and is said to have been one of Sissi's favourite palace features.

Peristyle of the Muses Hall
This hall, at the back of the palace, has an understated elegance. Its pillars and statues surround an inner courtyard and lead down some steps to the beautiful gardens.

Palace Collection of Paintings
The palace has a rich collection of paintings *(left)* by famous and lesser-known artists of the period. Among them are portraits of Sissi and Kaiser Wilhelm II, and *Achilles' Triumph* by the 18th century Austrian painter Frantz Mats.

5 Kaiser's Room

Known as Kaiser's Room *(left)*, the office of Kaiser Wilhelm II, the last emperor of Germany, is located on the ground floor of the palace. Displayed in the room are his personal belongings, including documents, furniture, portraits and a collection of medals.

6 Empress Elisabeth's Catholic Chapel

This tiny chapel *(right)*, with an icon of the Virgin Mary, is where Sissi is said to have prayed. It lies just off the palace's main entrance hall, and has a beautiful ceiling fresco.

7 Statues of Hera and Zeus

Princess Sissi adored Greek mythology and commissioned statues of gods to be placed around the palace. These include the statues of Hera *(right)* and Zeus, which stand at the foot of the marble staircase leading up to the first floor.

8 Statues of Goddesses in the Gardens

Statues of important Greek mythological figures also adorn the palace's gardens. Among them are the goddesses Artemis, the goddess of forests and hunting, who is seen standing upright and defiant, and Aphrodite, also known as Venus, the goddess of love and beauty.

9 Statue of the Dying Achilles

One of the most impressive statues in the gardens is the *Dying Achilles (below)*, by the 19th-century German sculptor Ernst Herter. The large bronze depicts Achilles trying to remove an arrow from his heel and forms the garden's centrepiece.

10 Kaiser's Bridge

This arched bridge was requested by Kaiser Wilhelm II to make a beach on the opposite side of the road more accessible. Parts of it were destroyed during World War II when Corfu was under German occupation, but it remains an important architectural landmark.

Achilles

Empress Elisabeth dedicated the Achílleion Palace to the mighty ancient warrior Achilles, famous for his role in the Battle of Troy, where he killed the Trojan hero Hector. As the story goes, the newly born Achilles was immersed in the River Styx by his mother. This ritual made him invincible, apart from the heel where she had held him. Achilles survived many fearsome battles, but at Troy the warrior Paris fatally shot him in his heel.

🔟 Mýrtou Bay Area, Kefalloniá

With its iconic white crescent-shaped beach, brilliant turquoise sea and mountainous backdrop, Mýrtou Bay has been voted one of the most beautiful bays in the world, and is, undoubtedly, the most photographed in the Ionians. The bay, often known as Myrtos, is flanked by two mountains, Agia Dynati and Kalon Oros. Located in the region of Pylaros, the bay can be reached by a road of hairpin bends that descends sharply from the scenic mountain village of Divarata. To the southeast of the bay lies the small yet bustling fishing village of Agia Effimia.

Forests carpeting the hills near Mýrtou Bay

🚫 The bay is protected from development. It offers visitors few facilities, other than basic refreshments.

• Map H4
• Mýrtou Bay: near Divarata and Siniόri, Kefalloniá

Top 10 Features
1. White Pebble Beach
2. Turquoise Sea
3. Sheer Cliffs
4. Silver Birch Forests
5. Panoramic Views
6. Diving and Snorkelling Coves
7. Mount Agia Dynati
8. Mount Kalon Oros
9. Divarata
10. Agia Effimia

White Pebble Beach
The dazzling white beach *(below)* has been formed over millennia by the erosion of the cliffs enclosing the bay. The rock debris was deposited on the beach and worn down by the sea to form pebbles.

Turquoise Sea
The sea's vivid blue colour is a result of the white-pebble seabed, which reflects the light. The colour is intensified by the deeply shelving beach and the motion of the sea, which picks up tiny pebbles as it hits the shore.

Sheer Cliffs
The soaring cliffs of Mýrtou Bay are a highlight of the area. Made up of calcite-rich limestone, the white cliffs contrast sharply with the deep blue colour of the sea.

Silver Birch Forests
The rural landscape on the hills above Mýrtou Bay is largely made up of forests of silver birch. This medium-sized deciduous tree can be recognized by its white trunk and pale green leaves, and is only found at higher altitudes on the island.

Panoramic Views
One of the best views of Mýrtou Bay is from above, along the well-signposted road from the village of Siniόri. There is a special viewing area for visitors that offers sweeping views of the white beach, the surrounding verdant countryside and the brilliant blue sea.

6 Diving and Snorkelling Coves

With its tiny coves, caves and rocks *(above)*, the bay provides a paradise for snorkelling and diving enthusiasts. However, caution must be taken as there are strong currents and the seabed drops dramatically, making the water especially deep at certain points.

7 Mount Agia Dynati

According to Greek lore, Agia Dynati was the rock that the Titan leader, Cronus, famously dropped to earth. After Lefkáda's Mount Elati and Kefalloniá's Mount Aino, Agia Dynati, at 1,100 m (4,000 ft), is the third-highest mountain in the Ionian islands.

8 Mount Kalon Oros

Along with Agia Dynati, Kalon Oros forms a dramatic backdrop to the bay. At around 900 m (3,000 ft), it offers superb views. From the mountain, look out for pretty villages where local crafts and traditions still thrive.

9 Divarata

The road to Mýtrou Bay descends from Divarata *(above)*, one of the small villages on Mount Agia Dynati. This scenic village has several tavernas and lies along the coast road from Kardakata to Fiskárdo.

10 Agia Effimia

Mýtrou Bay lies close to the traditional fishing village of Agia Effimia *(left)*, the capital of the Pylaros region. It is known for its lively nautical activity. From here, tour boats cruise along the coast, affording some of the best views of the bay.

Captain Corelli's Mandolin

Mýrtou Bay famously featured in the 2001 film *Captain Corelli's Mandolin*. The screenplay was adapted from British novelist Louis de Bernières' 1993 prize-winning novel of the same name. It chronicles the eviction of the Italians by the Germans in World War II *(see p31)*. Although both the film and the book have boosted tourism in the bay, it continues to retain its idyllic nature and is protected from indiscriminate development.

For more beaches in Kefalloniá **See pp32 and 82–3.**

Caves of Sámi, Kefalloniá

The massive Drogkaráti cave and the subterranean Melissáni cave, with its natural lake, are just two of Sámi's must-see attractions. The caves and underground lakes boast awesome natural wonders, including stalactites and stalagmites, which have formed over thousands of years. Sámi, a bustling and important harbour on the east coast of Kefalloniá (see p79), has suffered severely in earthquakes over the centuries, but the tremors have revealed entrances and passageways to these magnificent caves.

Small cafés en route to the caves, Kefalloniá

Try to get to the caves early to be ahead of the crowds arriving by coach.

Take bottled water or buy some from the cafés en route to the caves, or the nearby kiosk, as water is not available inside.

• Map H5
• Drogkaráti cave: open 8am–8pm daily; adm €2
• Melissáni cave: open 8am–8pm daily; adm €2

Top 10 Features

1. Drogkaráti Cave
2. Stalactites and Stalagmites
3. Royal Balcony
4. Chamber of Exaltation
5. Angalaki Cave
6. Zervati Cave
7. Melissáni Cave
8. Lake Melissáni
9. Aghia Theodori Cave
10. Aghia Eleousa Cave

Drogkaráti Cave
A geological wonder created by the erosion of rocks by water, this massive cave *(main image)* was discovered about 300 years ago following an earthquake that revealed its entrance. One of several Sámi caves, Drogkaráti is believed to be more than a million years old.

Stalactites and Stalagmites
Hundreds of subtly lit stalactites and stalagmites *(above)*, formed over millennia, give Drogkaráti cave an atmospheric feel. Some are broken, probably due to earthquakes, but most are still intact and continue to attract many visitors.

Royal Balcony
Creatively known as the Royal Balcony, this unique feature of the Drogkaráti cave is a natural rock platform on which visitors can stand and admire the amazing stalactites and stalag-mites, and look ahead to the cavern known as the Chamber of Exaltation.

Chamber of Exaltation
Also known as the Sala of Apotheosis, this huge chamber is said to have perfect acoustics and is often used for musical concerts. Its most famous performer was Maria Callas, the celebra-ted Greek soprano. The cave is accessed via a bridge over a lake.

5 Angalaki Cave
The largest of all the caves, the Angalaki cave can be found along the main road leading north out of Sámi. Among its fascinating features are enormous caverns, underground lakes and shelves along the walls formed by erosion of the rocks.

6 Zervati Cave
The Zervati cave has passages that descend deep down into the earth. Like Angalaki cave, it is one of the deepest in the Sámi area and has cavernous chambers and underground lakes, many with submerged stalactites and stalagmites.

7 Melissáni Cave
Discovered by Gianni Petrochilo, a speleologist, in 1951, this cave *(below)* is also called the Cave of Nymphs. It is said to have been the sanctuary of the god Pan and several nymphs. It is particularly famous for its turquoise lake that is lit by the sun through a hole in its roof.

8 Lake Melissáni
The underground lake *(below)* at the Melissáni cave is named after a nymph. It is fed from the streams of the cave system that follow a course to the sea. Excavations here have revealed artifacts that date back to the 4th century BC.

9 Aghia Theodori Cave
Aghia Theodori is one of the lesser-known caves of Sámi. It is made up of a deep shaft created in the bedrock that leads to a small underground saltwater lake, which is believed to be home to a variety of fish and subterranean foliage.

10 Aghia Eleousa Cave
Remarkable only for the fact that it was created by nature, this cave is neither deep nor large. However, it does empty into a salt-water lake thought to be connected to the underground stream network that originates at Katavothres and feeds Lake Melissáni.

Stalactites and Stalagmites
Stalactites thrive in a cave-like environment and hang from the ceiling of many of the Sámi caves. Stalactites are created by calcite and other mineral deposits found in rain that seeps through rock and solidifies when it reaches air. They grow at the rate of around 10 mm (0.3 inches) every 100 years. Stalagmites are the structures that are formed on the cave floor by drips from the stalactites above.

ᵀᴼᴾ10 Zákynthos Town

The elegant capital and principal port of the island of the same name, Zákynthos Town is characterized by its beautiful squares, such as the Plateia Solomoú, arcaded streets and attractive waterfront, where colourful fishing boats come in and out of the bustling harbour. Although the town dates back centuries, its buildings were all but destroyed in the 1953 earthquake that shook the Ionian islands. It has been sensitively rebuilt in a refreshing Venetian Neo-Classical style, in its original layout.

A busy outdoor café in Zákynthos Town

⊘ **Zákynthos is easy to navigate, as most of its main thoroughfares run parallel to the esplanade.**

• Museum of Solomós: Map L4; Plateia Ag Markou; 26950 48982; open 9am–2pm daily; adm €4
• Church of St Dionýsios: Map L6; Ag Dionýsiou
• Naval Museum of Zákynthos: Map K4; Bochali Hill; open 9am–2pm daily; adm €3
• Plateia Rouga: Map L5
• The Venetian Fortress: Map K4; Bochali Hill; 26950 48099; open summer: 8am–3pm Tue–Sun; winter: 8:30am–3pm Tue–Sun; adm €3
• Church of St Nikolaos on the Mole: Map M5; Plateia Solomoú
• Ecclesiastical Museum: Map L6; Church of St Dionýsios; open 9am–1pm, 2pm–9pm Tue–Sun; adm €2
• Lomvardou Street: Map M5

Top 10 Features

1. Museum of Solomós
2. Church of St Dionýsios
3. Venetian Bell Tower
4. Naval Museum of Zákynthos
5. Plateia Rouga
6. Venetian Fortress
7. Bochali Hill
8. Church of St Nikolaos on the Mole
9. Ecclesiastical Museum
10. Lomvardou Street

1 Museum of Solomós

An attractive museum in the heart of Zákynthos Town, the Museum of Solomós celebrates the lives of prominent Zákynthiot citizens, most notably the 19th-century poet Dionysios Solomós. It houses the poet's tomb and exhibits a rich collection of manuscripts.

2 Church of St Dionýsios

The impressive waterside Church of St Dionýsios *(below)* is dedicated to the patron saint of the island, whose body lies here in a silver coffin. The church houses icons and frescoes by the 19th-century Zákynthiot painters Doxaras and Koutouzis.

3 Venetian Bell Tower

The bell tower of the Church of St Dionýsios is one of the most photographed landmarks in Zákynthos Town. It is modelled on San Marco in Venice and was one of the few structures to have survived the earthquake of 1953.

4 Naval Museum of Zákynthos

Dedicated to the history of the Greek merchant navy, this museum has a large collection of instruments, uniforms and paintings from the 18th century to the present day. On display are interesting records of naval activity during the two world wars.

Plateia Rouga
The town's main thoroughfare, the Plateia Rouga (above) has side streets with graceful arches, colourful buildings, stylish shops and chic cafés where you can sit and watch the world go by.

Venetian Fortress
Overlooking the town, this mid-17th-century fortress (below) once played a key role in defending the town against invaders. Look out for the Lions of St Markos inscription above the entrance.

Bochali Hill
This hill is believed to be the site of the ancient acropolis Psofida, upon which the fort was built. Surrounded by pine forests, it offers splendid views of the pretty suburb of Zoodochos Pigi.

Church of St Nikolaos on the Mole
This delightful church, dating from the mid-16th century, is mentioned in history books as the site where St Dennis, an important saint from the island, served. It is Plateia Solomóu's oldest building.

Ecclesiastical Museum
Housed in the Monastery of St Dionýsios, next to the church here, this small museum (below) boasts a valuable collection of icons from the Monastery of Strofades, home to St Dionýsios in the 16th century.

Zákynthos Through the Ages
Zákynthos was named after the son of the Arcadian hero Dardanus, who was the son of the Greek god Zeus. When the island came under Venetian rule in the 15th century, its capital, Zákynthos Town, was developed. The French, Russians and British all left their stamp on the town until, in 1953, it was all but destroyed in a mighty earthquake.

Lomvardou Street
Known locally as Strata Marina, the esplanade that runs along the town's busy harbour has elegant buildings on one side and colourful boats bobbing in the water on the other. Ferries regularly ply from the port.

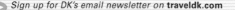

Byzantine Museum, Zákynthos Town

Occupying a prominent Neo-Classical building on the main square in Zákynthos Town, this exquisite museum is home to a breathtaking collection of ecclesiastical art, one of the finest in Greece. Founded in the late 1950s to house the fabulous icons and frescoes that were saved from the island's churches and monasteries after the 1953 earthquake, the museum opened its doors to the public in 1960.

Exterior of the Byzantine Museum, Plateia Solomóu

The museum organizes special tours for visitors with disabilities, and also provides good wheelchair access.

Have a drink and snack at one of the many cafés around Plateia Solomóu before entering this museum, as you will require some time to appreciate all the displays here.

- Map M4
- Plateia Solomóu, Zákynthos Town
- 26950 42714
- Open 8:30am–3pm Tue–Sun
- Adm adults: €3; concessions: €2; children under 18 and students: free

Top 10 Features

1. St Demetrios of Kola Templon
2. Model of Zákynthos Town
3. Descent from the Cross
4. Sanctuary Door from Panagiá Gavalousa
5. Birth of the Theotokos
6. Hellenic and Byzantine Sculpture Collection
7. Procession with the Relics of St Charalambos
8. Prophet David Portrait
9. Church of the Soter Wall Fresco
10. Panagiá the Amolyntos

1 St Demetrios of Kola Templon

Dating from 1690, this beautifully carved sanctuary screen *(main image)* once stood between the congregation and the inner sanctuary and altar of the Church of St Demetrios of Kola.

2 Model of Zákynthos Town

Capturing the layout and Venetian architecture of the pre-earthquake town to a scale of 1:500, local 20th-century artist Yianni Manesi made this fine model *(below)*.

3 Descent from the Cross

Painted by Nikolaos Kantounes, this 15th-century work from the Church of St Andreas of the Gardens is one of the museum's most famous exhibits. The painting shows Christ being lowered from the cross after his crucifixion.

4 Sanctuary door from Panagiá Gavalousa

Showing the apostles Paul on the right panel and Peter on the left, this well-preserved door, saved from the Panagiá (Virgin) Gavalousa Church, dates back to 1570.

5 Birth of the Theotokos

Saved from the Church of Phaneromene, this painting *(right)*, by the 18th-century artist Nikolaos Doxaras, shows St Anne with an infant watched over by angels.

6 Hellenic and Byzantine Sculpture Collection

The museum has an extensive collection of sculptures dating from Hellenic and Byzantine times. Subtly lit and displayed with informative labels, the exhibits include figurines, busts and architectural artifacts.

7 Procession with the Relics of St Charalambos

Artist Ioannes Korais painted this important work of art in 1756. It shows the social groups of the day in procession with an icon of one of the island's revered saints, St Charalambos. The painting was rescued from the church of the same name.

8 Prophet David Portrait

The 18th-century portrait of the Prophet David by Nikolaos Doxaras hangs in one of the main halls of the museum. Showing the prophet in profile, it is eye-catching because of its vibrant colours.

9 Church of the Soter Wall Fresco

This was rescued from the Church of the Soter (Saviour) in Zákynthos Town's Venetian Fortress *(see p21)*. Dating back to the 12th century, this fresco is one of the museum's oldest exhibits.

10 Panagiá the Amolyntos

The painting of the Panagiá (Virgin) with Child *(right)*, by the Cretan artist Emmanuel Tzanes, once adorned the walls of Zákynthos Town's Phaneromene Church. Considered an important example of 17th-century art, it is now one of the museum's main exhibits.

Museum Guide

The museum is divided into four main areas, all accessed through the front entrance hall. Area one displays wood carvings dating from the 16th to 19th centuries; area two is a small gallery of sculptures from the Hellenistic, early-Christian, Byzantine and post-Byzantine periods; area three exhibits wall paintings from the 12th to 13th and 17th to 18th centuries; and area four has Cretan and Ionian icons from the 15th to 16th centuries.

For more information on museums See pp38–9.

TOP 10 Lefkáda Town

Lying on a promontory around a natural harbour in Lefkáda's north, the island's capital has a modern appearance as a result of recurrent earthquake damage and the resulting reconstruction of its buildings. The town has a sophisticated, relaxed feel, and offers everything from tiny streets and squares to great waterfront restaurants and elegant shopping along Dorpfeld, its pedestrianized street. Life here revolves around the harbour area and lively marina. The town is linked to the Greek mainland by two small bridges over a channel.

Café on a narrow street, Lefkáda Town

🔵 **The Dorpfeld (the main shopping street) and the marina offer a wide range of cafés.**

- Map J1
- Sánta Mávra Fortress Ruins: Map J1; open 9am–3pm daily
- Archaeological Museum: Ag Sikelianou; 26450 21635; open summer: 8:30am–3pm Tue–Sun; winter: 8:30am–3pm daily; adm €2
- Orpheus Folklore Museum: T Stratou; 26450 33443; telephone for timings; adm €2
- Marina: Map J1
- Post-Byzantine Art Gallery: Rontogianni; 26450 22502; open 8:30am–1:30pm Tue–Sun; adm €2
- Monastery of Faneroménis: Frini; 26450 33443; open 8am–2pm and 4–8pm daily
- Phonograph Museum: Kalkani 14; 26450 33443; open summer: 10am–2pm and 7pm–midnight
- Mýlos Beach: Map H1
- Agios Ioannis Beach: Map J1

Top 10 Features

1. Colourful Architecture
2. Sánta Mávra Fortress Ruins
3. Archaeological Museum
4. Orpheus Folklore Museum
5. The Marina
6. Post-Byzantine Art Gallery
7. Monastery of Faneroménis
8. Phonograph Museum
9. Mýlos Beach
10. Agios Ioannis Beach

Colourful Architecture

Lefkáda Town is full of character. After the 1948 earthquake, which destroyed most of the town's original buildings, homes were rebuilt with timber frames covered with colourful metal sheets.

Sánta Mávra Fortress Ruins

Dominating the skyline near the channel are the ruins of the 14th-century castle of Sánta Mávra *(below)*, which was built to defend the town.

Archaeological Museum

Although the town looks relatively modern, it has a long and rich history. Its Archaeological Museum displays artifacts *(left)* unearthed from here and villages all over the island that date as far back as the early Bronze Age.

Orpheus Folklore Museum

Founded by the local Music and Literature Association, this small but exquisite museum houses a fabulous collection of traditional clothes worn by the Lefkádites for centuries. It also dispays textiles, looms and old photographs.

5 The Marina
Located on the town's east side, Lefkáda marina *(right)* is one of the largest and best equipped in the Ionians. It has bars, restaurants and shops, and offers all the facilities required by yachtsmen for berthing their vessels.

6 Post-Byzantine Art Gallery
Housed in a classical building, this art gallery is part of the town's hlibrary. It has books, manuscripts and a superb collection of post-Byzantine art and icons dating from the 17th to the 19th centuries.

7 Monastery of Faneroménis
Set high on a hill overlooking Lefkáda's harbour, this monastery *(below)* was founded in the 17th century. The present building is, however, more recent. Its ecclesiastical museum has many icons, the oldest of which is from the 15th century.

8 Phonograph Museum
This museum *(below)* has an unusual, privately owned collection of antique radios and gramophones, which date from a bygone age. There are musical instruments and sheet music, plus a range of personal items, such as gems and coins.

9 Mýlos Beach
For a great day trip from Lefkáda Town head to the beautiful Mýlos beach which is nestled in a scenic lagoon. The beach can be accessed by boat or over the headland west of the town. One of the abandoned windmills overlooking the beach here is now a café.

10 Agios Ioannis Beach
Lying just 2 km (1 mile) outside Lefkáda Town, Agios Ioannis, a beautiful stretch of sand, is one of the finest beaches on the island. The sand is golden and the sea a vivid turquoise. With a breeze blowing on most days, the beach has become well known as a windsurfing paradise.

Traditional Dress
Greece has many variations of traditional attire. Lefkádite men traditionally wear a *bourzana*, comprising short pants and a white shirt. Women wear a full dress, called a *katolo*. These are no longer worn everyday, but can be seen at festivals. Lefkáda is also known for its rich silk dresses worn by brides on their wedding day, and the traditional groom's costume of felt trousers, known as *vraka*, a white shirt and a waistcoat, known as a *geleki*.

Lefkáda's famous wine and outstanding needlecraft, known as *karsaniki velonia*, make good souvenirs.

Sailing Around the Ionians

The Ionian Sea, with its beautiful vistas and numerous natural harbours, offers some of the finest sailing in the Mediterranean. Enthusiasts can join organized flotillas, hire a yacht or take their own vessel around the islands. Particularly popular with yachtsmen are Corfu and Lefkáda, which has many satellite islands, such as scenic Meganísi (see p72). Other options are to sail around Paxí, Kefalloniá, Ithaki or Zákynthos, or between the islands. The Ionians offer a good choice of marinas and more informal anchorages.

Jetty offering boats for hire, Paleokastrítsa, Corfu

🌀 All the Ionian marinas have a good choice of restaurants and cafés.

- Gouvia Marina: Map C3; Tzavros, Corfu; 26610 91900
- Port Gäios Marina: Map B5; Paxí; 26620 32259
- Limin Kerkira Marina: Map C1; Corfu; 26610 32655
- Lefkáda Marina: Map J1; East Berth, Lefkáda Town, Lefkáda; 26450 26645
- Port Zákynthos Marina: Map M6; Zákynthos; 26950 28117
- Frikes Marina: Map G4; Ithaki;
- Argostóli Marina: Map G5; Kefalloniá;
- Sámi Marina: Map H5; Kefalloniá;
- Fiskárdo Marina: Map H4; Kefalloniá;
- Póros Marina: Map J6; Kefalloniá

Top 10 Features

1. Gouvia Marina, Corfu
2. Port Gäios Marina, Paxí
3. Limin Kerkira Marina, Corfu
4. Lefkáda Marina, Lefkáda
5. Port Zákynthos Marina, Zákynthos Town
6. Frikes Marina, Ithaki
7. Argostóli Marina, Kefalloniá
8. Sámi Marina, Kefalloniá
9. Fiskárdo Marina, Kefalloniá
10. Póros Marina, Kefalloniá

1 Gouvia Marina, Corfu

Lying about 6 km (4 miles) outside Corfu Town, Gouvia *(above)* is the main port of call for yachtsmen sailing around Corfu. Fully equipped, it can cater for around 1,200 yachts.

2 Port Gäios Marina, Paxí

Set in Paxí's prettiest harbour, Port Gäios *(below)* can berth yachts up to 6 m (20 ft) long. Facilities are few, but the waters here are a joy to sail.

3 Limin Kerkira Marina, Corfu

Located conveniently near the airport, the picturesque Limin Kerkira Marina has room for yachts of up to 50 m (164 ft) long. This well-equipped marina offers a good selection of facilities for both resident and visiting yachtsmen.

4 Lefkáda Marina, Lefkáda

This marina has stern or alongside berths for over 600 yachts. Maximum water depth is 4 m (13 ft). It offers sailors a wide range of facilities, including a chandlery and refuelling station, and is the ideal base for sailing trips around the coast of mainland Greece.

5 Port Zákynthos Marina, Zákynthos Town

One of the largest marinas in the Ionians, Port Zákynthos Marina *(above)* offers a range of facilities, from bars to nautical equipment. This great stop-off point is set within the town's main harbour.

9 Fiskárdo Marina, Kefalloniá

With a backdrop of Fiskárdo's delightful 18th-century Venetian houses that survived the 1953 earthquake, this well-equipped marina *(below)* is a great place to spend some time in between passages.

Póros Marina, Kefalloniá 10

Protected by a sea wall, Póros Marina *(right)* offers a safe haven for resident and visiting yachtsmen. Offering several facilities, including a restaurant and even a bank, it is an ideal place to stop off while sailing along Kefallonia's coast.

6 Frikes Marina, Ithaki

Located on Ithaki's east coast, the modest Frikes Marina *(main image)* only has room for small vessels, but is an ideal base for sailing around the island. The marina welcomes visiting yachtsmen and offers basic necessities.

7 Argostóli Marina, Kefalloniá

Facilities at this marina *(below)* include a crane and boat repair, plus a restaurant. It is possible to sail along the coast or take to the open sea from this marina.

8 Sámi Marina, Kefalloniá

The gateway to Kefalloniá, Sámi lies close to local amenities. Its sheltered position makes it a good stop-off point if the weather deteriorates.

Winds and Tides

The Ionians have one of the mildest climates of all the Greek island groups, and rarely does the wind speed hit anything more than a 4 on the Beaufort scale during the summer months. The Ionian Sea tends to be calmer in the mornings, with the Mediterranean *maïstro* wind blowing through most afternoons. The rise and fall of the tides is generally gentle and the surface currents tend to be weak.

The Ionians are popular for snorkelling and diving, and many companies offering trips operate out of the marinas.

Left **Napoleon Bonaparte** Right **Corfu Port under British protection**

TOP 10 Moments in History

1 Colonization by the Peloponnesians (8000 BC)

One of the earliest landmarks in the history of the Ionian islands was their colonization by the Peloponnesians and by the inhabitants of the island of Euboea, known today as Evvoia. These early settlers are believed to have arrived in the Ionians in around the mid-8th century BC. Few remains of these settlements exist today.

2 Peloponnesian War (431–404 BC)

Unrest between the residents of Corfu, allies of the Athens empire, and their colonizers, the Corinthians, triggered the Peloponnesian War between the Athens and Sparta empires. Harmony with the signing of the Peace of Nicias treaty in 421 BC was short-lived. The war concluded with a mighty battle at Aegospotami.

3 Subjugation by Rome (197 BC)

The Ionian islands were a part of the Macedonian empire from the 4th century BC until 197 BC, when Greece was subjugated by Rome. The islands enjoyed a period of peace as part of the Eastern Roman Empire until Venetian crusaders arrived in 1204, after the invasion of Constantinople in the Fourth Crusade.

4 Venetian Rule (1204–1797)

The Republic of Venice took control of the Ionians from 1204. This was a key period in the history of the islands – it was due to strong Venetian fortifications that they were able to escape occupation during the Ottoman invasion of Greece. As a result, the islands remained Christian.

5 Septinsular Republic (1800–1807)

The islands became a part of France when Napoleon Bonaparte conquered Venice in 1797. The next year, the Russians, under the distinguished naval commander Admiral Ushakov, evicted the French and established the Russo-Ottoman Septinsular Republic.

6 French Occupation (1807–1814)

The islands were reclaimed by France in 1807. Although organized into *départements* under the previous French rule, they were now considered part of the

A 19th-century depiction of the Peloponnesian War

Preceding pages **An elegant row of statues and columns at the Achílleion Palace, Corfu**

Illyrian Provinces. The islands remained strategic locations to the French until Napoleon's empire collapsed in 1814.

British Protectorate (1814–1864)

The 1815 Treaty of Paris placed the Ionian islands under British protection. The British High Commissioner and an elected assembly worked together to improve the islands' infrastructure.

Union with Greece (1864)

Ionian residents wanted a union with Greece after its independence in 1830. Britain agreed to relinquish the islands, provided it could still use Corfu Port, and the Ionians became provinces of the Kingdom of Greece in 1864.

German tanks entering Greece in 1941

Axis Occupation (1941)

During World War II, the Axis alliance, which included Germany, Japan and Italy, took control of Greece. The Italians claimed sole power in 1941, but the Germans evicted them in 1943 and killed most of the Jewish population.

Major Earthquake (1953)

The most significant event in the recent history of the islands was the devastating earthquake of 1953. It recorded 7.1 on the Richter scale and destroyed entire towns on Zákynthos and Kefalloniá. Many towns have since been rebuilt to earthquake-proof standards.

Top 10 Historical Figures

1 Napoleon Bonaparte
Napoleon (1769–1821), later Emperor Napoleon I, defeated the Venetian Republic in 1797.

2 Sir Thomas Maitland
Sir Thomas (1759–1824) was the first British Lord High Commissioner of the Ionians, from 1815 to 1823.

3 Sir Frederick Adam
Sir Frederick (1781-1853) held the office of the second Lord High Commissioner of the Ionians, from 1823 to 1831.

4 Dionýsios Solomós
Poet and patron saint of Zákynthos, Solomós (1798–1857) wrote *Hymn to Freedom*, the Greek national anthem.

5 William Gladstone
British Prime Minister Gladstone (1809–1898) was instrumental in handing over the Ionians to Greece in 1864.

6 Empress Elisabeth of Austria
Elisabeth (1837–1898), Empress of Bavaria and later of Austria, had Corfu's Achílleion Palace built in the 1890s.

7 King George I
The King of Greece, King George I (1845–1913), had his summer residence at Corfu's Mon Repos Estate.

8 Kaiser Wilhelm II
The last German emperor, Wilhelm II (1859–1941) bought the Achílleion Palace after the death of Elisabeth of Austria.

9 Duke of Edinburgh
Grandson of King George I, Prince Philip is the current Duke of Edinburgh and husband of Queen Elizabeth II. He was born in Corfu in 1921.

10 Gerald Durrell
Durrell's (1925–1995) classic memoir, *My Family and Other Animals* (1956), recalls his Corfiot childhood.

Left **The popular Antísamos beach, Kefalloniá** Right **Windmills on Mýlos beach, Lefkáda**

TOP 10 Beaches

The idyllic Platýs Yalos beach, Kefalloniá

Platýs Yalos and Makrýs Yalos Beaches, Kefalloniá
These two beaches lie side by side at Lassí on Kefalloniá's west coast, south of Argostóli *(see p79)*. Both are long and sandy, with a scattering of rocks. The sea here is especially safe for swimmers, and water-sports enthusiasts can be seen water-skiing and windsurfing *(see p83)*.

Xi Beach, Kefalloniá
Famous for its fine deep-red sand, Xi beach is located opposite Argostóli and south of Lixoúri *(see p82)* on the Pallikí peninsula. Rows of bright parasols provide shade from the sun here, and cliffs form a spectacular backdrop *(see p83)*.

Antísamos Beach, Kefalloniá
One of several Kefallonián beaches that featured in the 2001 film *Captain*

Corelli's Mandolin (see p17), Antísamos is a beautiful beach located near the east-coast town of Sámi *(see p79)*. This white shingle beach looks out across the water to Ithaki opposite and is popular with locals. It has a backdrop of hills and forest *(see p83)*.

Arillas Beach, Corfu
Located on the northwest coast of Corfu, near the town of Agios Stefanos, Arillas beach is a long stretch of soft sand and is as picturesque as it is quiet. The sea breaks against several small islands and islets that lie off its shoreline *(see p62)*.

Yaliskari Beach, Corfu
The idyllic beach of Yaliskari is the prettiest in a necklace of quiet, sandy coves along Corfu's west coast; its neighbours include Ermones, Pélekas *(see p61)*, Myrtiótissa *(see p62)* and Agios Gordios. The scenic coastline along Yaliskari is dotted with rock formations, and is a popular camping spot *(see p62)*.

The picturesque Pórto Katsiki beach, Lefkáda

→ *Beaches on the Ionians are often remote, so be sure to take refreshments with you.*

beach, which is surrounded by lush vegetation and tall cliffs, is considered one of the best on the island. This stunning beach is horseshoe-shaped and has golden sand and interesting rock formations that are fun to explore (see p71).

Vromi cove, tucked into the western coast of Zákynthos

Vrika Beach, Antipaxí
One of the most popular beaches on Antipaxí, Vrika is characterized by its golden sand and clear turquoise sea. Yachts and motor boats can often be seen anchored a little way off this pretty cove, while their owners swim in the warm water (see p62).

Voutoumi Beach, Antipaxí
Sandy Voutoumi beach lies on the eastern coast of Antipaxí. It is linked to Vrika beach by a pathway that passes by the vineyards and olive and citrus groves that dominate the island's landscape. The beach offers fabulous views of the coastline. Trees here provide shelter from the sun (see p62).

Mýlos Beach, Lefkáda
The sandy Mýlos beach, with its picturesque windmills, is a great place to go if you wish to escape the crowds. It lies near the lively fishing village of Agios Nikitas (see p72), from where you can walk over the headland to the beach or take a boat along the coastline (see p25).

Pórto Katsiki Beach, Lefkáda
Located not far from the windsurfer's paradise of Vasilikí (see p70), Lefkáda's Pórto Katsiki

Vromi Cove, Zákynthos
This delightful cove on the west coast of Zákynthos is a photographer's dream. Like the other scenic coves dotted along this stretch of coastline, such as Exo Chora (see p96) and Navagio beach, also known as Shipwreck Bay (see p92), Vromi overlooks a pristine turquoise sea and has soft sand the colour of honey (see p96).

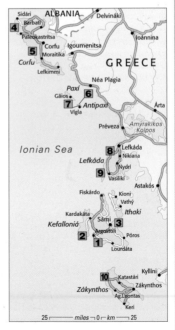

Left **View from the top of Mount Pantokrátor, Corfu** Right **Korisíon Lagoon, Corfu**

Natural Wonders

1 Small Islands
More than 30 small islands lie off the coastlines of the main islands. Most are rocky and bare, but some have scenic villages and beaches. Vidos, in Corfu's harbour, and Dia *(see p82)*, off Kefalloniá's south coast, are two of the prettiest. The largest is Meganísi *(see p72)*, off Lefkáda's east coast.

2 Mount Pantokrátor, Corfu
Mount Pantokrátor, whose name means "the Almighty", dominates northeast Corfu. It rises so steeply that its peak, at over 900 m (3,000 ft), is less than 3 km (2 miles) from the coast. A series of hairpin bends lead to its summit, which affords spectacular views in every direction *(see p58)*.

3 Korisíon Lagoon, Corfu
A massive stretch of water separated from the sea by sand dunes and beaches, this lagoon is a fabulous haven for wildlife, such as sandpipers and egrets. The freshwater lake is around 5 km (3 miles) long and surrounded by lush vegetation *(see p58)*.

4 Kastanitha Cave, Paxí
Kastanitha cave is one of Paxí's most striking natural features. Lying on the northwest coast near Lákka, the 180-m- (590-ft-) tall cave is a wondrous sight as you approach it by boat.
⬥ Map A5 • Near Lákka, Paxí

5 Blue Caves, Zákynthos
Located at Cape Skinári on the northernmost tip of Zákynthos, the Blue Caves are a delightful sight – the water between the arches of the caves appear bright blue when the sun shines in. Take a boat from Agios Nikólaos village and sail along the coastline for the best views of the caves *(see p91)*.

A ferry off Meganísi island near Lefkáda

The azure water of Lake Melissáni, Kefalloniá

9 Lake Melissáni, Kefalloniá

Fed by a system of caves, this underground lake is a mix of sea water and freshwater. The mineral content gives the lake its deep blue colour. It was named after the nymph Melissáni when ancient artifacts with images of legendary figures were discovered here *(see pp18–19)*.

6 The Spring of Aretousa, Ithaki

The Spring of Aretousa is believed to be the one described by Homer in *The Odyssey*, where Odysseus met Eumaeus. Whether this is true or not, the ravine-side walk towards the spring is beautiful, if a little challenging for anyone afraid of heights.
🔊 *Map J4 • S of Vathý, Ithaki*

7 Drogkaráti Cave, Kefalloniá

This huge and enchanting cave, located at Sámi, is believed to be more than a million years old. Its interiors are covered in stalactites and stalagmites. The Royal Balcony and the Chamber of Exaltation, which boasts such superb acoustics that it is now often used as a venue for operatic performances, are two particularly breathtaking features of the cave *(see p18)*.

8 Katavothres Tunnel, Kefalloniá

Sea water disappears underground via this natural tunnel near Argostóli and then makes its way through an elaborate subterranean cave system across the island to Lake Melissáni *(see pp18–19)*. The tunnel was discovered in the 1950s during experiments conducted with dye mixed with the lake's water.
🔊 *Map G5 • Katavothres, Kefalloniá*

10 Grava Gardikiou, Corfu

Of all the the cave formations in the Ionians, Grava Gardikiou is particularly noted for its ancient history. Finds from the Upper Palaeolithic period, around 20,000 BC, indicate that this rock shelter may have been a site where hunters gathered.
🔊 *Map C5 • Southwest coast, Corfu*

The landscape of the Ionian islands is characterized by an abundance of olive trees and vineyards.

Left **Ruins of the Temple of Apollo, Lefkáda** Right **The sea god, Poseidon, in Greek mythology**

Myths and Legends

1 The Odyssey, Ithaki
According to legend, Ithaki was the home of the ancient Greek hero Odysseus, depicted vividly in Homer's epic poem *The Odyssey*. The great warrior returned here from Troy to be reunited with his love, Penelope.

2 Poseidon, Paxí
Legend has it that Paxí was joined to Corfu in the past, but was separated when the sea god Poseidon (Neptune) became enraged and dealt a blow to the region with his trident (three-pronged spear). One island became two, so the story goes, and now the island of Paxí lies to the south of Corfu.

3 Corinthians, Lefkáda
In ancient times, a narrow strip of land connected Lefkáda to the mainland. It is said that the Corinthians, who established Leukas city – modern-day Lefkáda Town – wanted complete control of the territory, so they destroyed the isthmus to create the island of Lefkáda.

4 St John of Antzousis and Paul the Apostle, Lefkáda
The small church dedicated to St John of Antzousis is believed to be the site where Paul the Apostle, a keen traveller around the Mediterranean, preached Christianity. ◈ *Map J1 • W of Lefkáda Town, Lefkáda*

Odysseus and his dog, Argus

5 Agios Anargyroi, Lefkáda
This delightful church is one of the numerous centuries-old churches that can be found in Lefkáda Town. While other Lefkádite churches, such as St Nicholas and St Menas, were patronized by the wealthy, Agios Anargyroi was a refuge to the poor and "Penniless Saints" after whom it was named. ◈ *Map J1 • Lefkáda Town, Lefkáda*

6 Apollo Leukatas, Lefkáda
The god Apollo – referred to as Apollo Leukatas by the people of the ancient city of Leukas (modern-day Lefkáda Town) – had such a strong cult following in ancient times that it still survives in folklore today. He was worshipped at a once-splendid sanctuary near Cavo Nira *(see p71)*.

7 Sappho, Lefkáda
The Greek poet Sappho was born around 620 BC. It is said that she fell in love with an ugly

Sappho and Phaon (1809) by D J Louis

boatman, Phaon, whom the goddess Aphrodite transformed into a handsome man. When he rejected Sappho, she was broken-hearted and jumped to her death from the cliffs near Cape Lefkáda.

Bay of Polis, Ithaki
Popular with visitors today, the Bay of Polis (see p82) is said to have been a place of worship in ancient times. Loizos cave, where age-old graffiti and artifacts have been discovered, was at the centre of the worship of the legendary goddesses Athena, Artemis and Hera.

Hermit Gerasímos, Kefalloniá
The patron saint of Kefalloniá, St Gerasímos, lived as a hermit in the Agios Gerasímos cave. Close by is a convent founded by the saint in the 16th century, and the Monastery of St Gerasímos (see p41), which houses the saint's remains.

Monastery of St Gerasímos, Kefalloniá

St Francis of Assisi, Kefalloniá
St Francis of Assisi is said to have founded the beautiful Monastery of the All Holy Mother of God of Sisies, or the Moní Theotókou Sisíon, in the 13th century. A friar of the Roman Catholic church and founder of the Franciscans, the saint preached Christianity across the Mediterranean. ◈ Map H6 • Near Lourdáta, Kefalloniá

Top 10 Ancient Sites

1 Palaio Frourio, Corfu
This 16th-century fortress dominates Corfu Town's skyline (see p8).

2 St Kerkyra Basilica, Corfu
Now ruined, this church was an important place of worship in the 5th century AD. (see p13).

3 Palaiokastró, Kefalloniá
Mycenaean fortifications and citadel remains have been unearthed at this ancient city near Lixoúri (see p80).

4 Analipsis Hill, Corfu
Remains of a 6th-century-BC Doric temple stand on this hill. ◈ Map D4 • Analipsis Hill, Corfu Town, Corfu

5 Angelokastro, Corfu
Located near Krini, this was the site of the important 13th-century Angelokastro fortress. ◈ Map A3 • Krini, Corfu

6 Skála, Kefalloniá
A 3rd-century-BC Roman villa at Skála houses some exceptionally well-preserved floor mosaics (see p80).

7 Palaiochóra, Ithaki
Once Ithaki's capital, this medieval site includes ruins of stone houses and churches. ◈ Map J4 • Palaiochóra, Ithaki

8 Hypapanti, Paxí
Legend says that this sea cave was a Byzantine church dedicated to the Presentation of Christ in the Temple. ◈ Map A5 • Hypapanti, Paxí

9 Cavo Nira Sanctuary, Lefkáda
In Greek folklore, this ancient sanctuary was the shrine of Apollo Leukatas (see p71).

10 Monastery of the Revealed Saints, Kefalloniá
This monastery, now in ruins, retains some important post-Byzantine wall frescoes. ◈ Map H5 • Sámi, Kefalloniá

For information on the history of the Ionians See pp30–31.

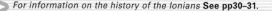

Left **Antivouniotissa Museum, Corfu** Right **Displays in the Archaeological Museum, Lefkáda**

Museums and Galleries

1 Archaeological Museum, Lefkáda

With a collection of artifacts dating from the early Bronze Age, this museum explores Lefkáda's ancient history. Its exhibits were excavated from sites around the island, including Kariotes, outside Lefkáda Town, and Nydrí, on the east coast *(see p24)*.

2 Orpheus Folklore Museum, Lefkáda

The exhibits in this superb museum in Lefkáda Town chronicle everyday life on the island. On display are textiles, household items, tools and even a baby's crib. One room has been transformed to resemble a local home. All exhibits here are believed to be from the 19th–20th centuries *(see p24)*.

3 Antivouniotissa Museum, Corfu

This museum contains a fabulous collection of Byzantine and post-Byzantine treasures and ecclesiastical artifacts dating back some five centuries. It is located in the Church of Panagia Antivouniotissa, one of the oldest churches on the Ionian islands *(see p9)*.

4 Archaeological Museum, Corfu

The sculptured Gorgon Medusa frieze, found at the ancient site of the Temple of Artemis and dating back to 590 BC, is a highlight of this great museum. The 7th-century BC Lion of Menecrates sculpture is also displayed here *(see pp10–11)*.

Byzantine Museum icon, Zákynthos

5 Museum of Solomós, Zákynthos

Dedicated to famous Zákynthians, including the 19th-century poets Dionýsios Solomós, who wrote the Greek National Anthem, and Andreas Kalvos, this museum has a lavish collection of manuscripts and displays of personal possessions. It also houses the tomb of Solomós *(see p20)*.

6 Byzantine Museum, Zákynthos

The museum has a fabulous collection of ecclesiastical art comprising pieces that were saved from the island's churches and monasteries following the 1953 earthquake. Displays include icons, paintings, templons (sanctuary screens) and even a model of the elegant pre-earthquake town *(see pp22–3)*.

7 Naval Museum, Zákynthos

Reports and letters written during the two world wars, with details of the Greek merchant navy's wartime activities, are the highlights of this museum. Also on display are uniforms, paintings, instruments and artifacts rescued from old ships, some dating back to the 18th century *(see p20)*.

8 Vathý Archaeological Museum, Ithaki

On display at this fascinating museum are ceramic pots and vases, metal tools and household items from the geometric period of Greek art (9th to 7th centuries BC) to Roman times. Many of these artifacts were found during digs at Piso Aetós (see p81). The most significant exhibit here is an intricately decorated vase with inscriptions mentioning the goddesses Athena and Hera.
Ⓢ Map J4 • Vathý, Ithaki • 26740 32200 • Open 9am–1pm daily • Adm

9 Stavrós Archaeological Museum, Ithaki

This compact museum is housed in a single room of a beautiful old village house, but what it lacks in size is more than made up for in its exhibits. Some of the items on display are believed to date from ancient times, when the nearby Bay of Polis (see p82) was a major port.
Ⓢ Map H4 • Stavrós, Ithaki • 6945 840055 • Open 9am–2:30pm Tue–Sun

10 Museum of Asiatic Art, Corfu

Housed in the Palace of St Michael and St George, this museum has over 11,000 pieces of Chinese, Korean and Japanese weapons, furniture, furnishings, ceramics and miniatures amassed by Corfiot diplomat Grigórios Mános (see p9).

Museum of Asiatic Art, Corfu

Top 10 Unusual Museums

1 Phonograph Museum, Lefkáda
A stunning private collection of old records and phonographs is housed here (see p25).

2 Paper Money Museum, Corfu
Notes from Corfu's British, German, Italian and Greek eras are displayed here (see p45).

3 Museum of Mesi, Corfu
This rural house has been converted into a museum.
Ⓢ Map C4 • Sinarades, Corfu • 26610 54962

4 Patounis Soap Factory, Corfu
See olive oil soap being made and stamped in the traditional way here. Ⓢ Map P2 • Corfu Town, Corfu • 26610 39806

5 Lace Museum, Zákynthos
This museum is worth a visit if you are in the village.
Ⓢ Map K1 • Volímes, Zákynthos

6 Monastery of Faneroménis Museum, Lefkáda
Ecclesiastical art is displayed at this museum (see p25).

7 Karya Museum, Lefkáda
Exhibits here showcase the way of life of Lefkádite mountain villagers. Ⓢ Map H2 • Kariá, Lefkáda • 26450 41590

8 Folk Museum, Paxí
Each room here tells Paxí's history. Ⓢ Map B5 • Gäios, Paxí • 26620 32566

9 Shell Museum, Corfu
Thousands of shells and marine objects are exhibited here. Ⓢ Map D4 • Benítses Harbour, Corfu

10 Maritime Museum, Zákynthos
This museum displays unique maritime objects. Ⓢ Map L2 • Tsilíví, Zákynthos

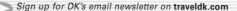

Left **Cathedral of the Virgin, Ithaki** Right **Monastery of St Gerasímos, Kefalloniá**

Cathedrals and Monasteries

1 Cathedral of the Virgin Spiliotissa, Corfu

Dedicated to one of the island's revered saints, St Theodora, this Greek Orthodox cathedral dates from the 16th century. Its carved-wood iconostasis – a screen that divides the sanctuary and the nave – is well-preserved and covered with icons of the Virgin. ⊗ *Map P4 • Corfu Town, Corfu*

2 Platytera Monastery, Corfu

Famous for housing the tomb of the first Governor of Greece – the Corfiot Ioánnis Kapodístrias who held office from 1872 to 1831 – this monastery dates from the 18th century. Nearby, there is a statue of the governor. ⊗ *Map N1 • Corfu Town, Corfu*

3 Monastery of the Virgin of Vlacherna, Corfu

Set on the islet of Vlacherna and linked to Corfu by a small bridge, the Monastery of the Virgin of Vlacherna dates back centuries. The distinctive white building lies on the edge of a beautiful lagoon known as Chalikopoulos. ⊗ *Map D4 • Kanóni, Corfu*

4 Cathedral of the Virgin, Ithaki

Dedicated to the Virgin Mary, this Greek Orthodox cathedral is beautiful. Its carved stonework and bell tower, which date from 1820, are well preserved and the 18th-century iconostasis is one of the finest examples in the Ionians. ⊗ *Map J4 • Vathý, Ithaki*

5 Monastery of the Virgin Hodegetria, Lefkáda

Built in 1420, this monastery is the oldest on Lefkáda and noted for its traditional 15th-century design, characterized by a single aisle and austere exterior. The intricate craftsmanship of its timber roof is mesmerizing. ⊗ *Map J1 • Lefkáda Town outskirts, Lefkáda*

6 Monastery of St John of Lagada, Zákynthos

Mountains provide an impressive backdrop to this remote monastery, which lies beside Alykés bay. It is located near the island's largest village, Katastári, and has a delightful chapel with an iconostasis and wall frescoes. ⊗ *Map L2 • Katastári, Zákynthos*

Monastery of the Virgin of Vlacherna, Corfu

7 Monastery of the Virgin Anafonítria, Zákynthos

Home to St Dionýsios from the 16th to 17th centuries, this remote monastery lies at Anafonítria *(see p92)* in the foothills of Mount

A particularly good time to visit Corfu is during Easter, when locals celebrate with festivities and colourful street displays.

Vrahiónas. Its small chapel is noted for its well-preserved gold-covered iconostasis and icons.
🔊 *Map K2 • Anafonítria, Zákynthos*

8 Katharon Monastery, Ithaki
At an altitude of around 600 m (2,000 ft), Katharon is one of the highest monasteries in the islands. It lies on Mount Niritos, not far from the small village of Anogi. Remote and beautiful, the monastery is dedicated to the Virgin Mary. 🔊 *Map J4 • Anogi, Ithaki*

Katharon Monastery, Ithaki

9 Cathedral of the Evangelistria, Kefalloniá
An enchanting Greek Orthodox building, the Cathedral of the Evangelistria is a relatively new landmark in Argostóli, the capital of Kefalloniá. It was built in 1957 and is significant because of its intricate icons and iconostasis, all the work of celebrated local artist Theodoroi Poulakis.
🔊 *Map G5 • Argostóli, Kefalloniá*

10 Monastery of St Gerasímos, Kefalloniá
Dedicated to Kefalloniá's patron saint, St Gerasímos *(see p37)*, this monastery lies at the foothills of Mount Ainos, near Argostóli. The saint's remains are housed here. The biannual Litany of St Gerasímos festival *(see p52)* revolves around this monastery.
🔊 *Map G5 • Argostóli, Kefalloniá*

Top 10 Religious Festivals

1 Epiphany
January sees Epiphany festivities take place, when the waters are blessed at sea-fronts around the islands.

2 Shrove Monday
Signalling the start of Lent, Orthodox Shrove Monday is marked with a religious service at the beginning of March.

3 Lent
Most Ionians mark this period of penance by observing abstinance to commemorate Jesus's fasting before Easter.

4 Good Friday and Easter Monday
Bombola lights line the routes of all the Easter processions that take place on the Ionians.

5 Easter
The most sacred religious festival in the Ionians, Easter is a time for families to celebrate with services and a feast.

6 Procession of the Icon of the Sisies Monastery, Kefalloniá
Kefalloniá marks Easter Monday with this important religious Procession of the icon of the Sisies Monastery.

7 Pentecost
Also known as the Feast of Weeks, Pentecost marks the descent of the Holy Ghost and is celebrated with church services and family feasts.

8 Dormition of the Virgin
The Dormition of the Virgin takes place on 15 August and is marked with church services.

9 Christmas
Christmas is marked with festivals, prayers and the giving of gifts on Christmas Eve.

10 Traditional Festivals
Each island's patron saint is celebrated with traditional festivals of dance, music and feasts held in village squares.

➤ *For more information on festivals and events* **See pp52–3.**

Left **Eleftherotria Monastery near Lagópodo, Zákynthos** Right **Pélekas, Corfu**

Picturesque Villages

Kávos, Corfu
Although Kávos beach is a bustling tourist spot, the village of Kávos is quiet and charming. The surrounding forests are great for walks and, on a clear day, boast views out over to Paxí. Originally a fishing village, Kávos still retains many of its old stone houses *(see p61)*.

Pélekas, Corfu
Perched on the top of a hill, Pélekas is one of the prettiest villages in the Ionians, and offers a fantastic view out over Glyfáda beach to the sea. The sunsets here are breathtaking *(see p61)*.

Fiskárdo, Kefalloniá
The quintessential picture-postcard village, Fiskárdo is a popular holiday destination. Having survived the devastating earthquake of 1953, the village retains its centuries-old buildings painted in soft pastel shades that line the picturesque harbourside.

It is a favourite haunt of yachtsmen, as well as gourmet diners and serious souvenir shoppers *(see p80)*.

Englouvi, Lefkáda
Located roughly at the centre of Lefkáda, Englouvi is the highest village on the island. With beautiful stone buildings and fields of crops, the village exudes charm. It is well known for its lentil crops – the seeds go into many local dishes – and its delicious, fresh honey. Nearby is the village of Kariá *(see p72)*, famous for its many shops selling lace embroidery. **⊙** *Map H2 • S of Kariá, Lefkáda*

Agios Petros, Lefkáda
Agios Petros is one of the tiny villages that you come across after negotiating a series of hair-pin bends along the road that traverses the foothills of Mount Elati. The views from this road are fantastic. You can reach the

The harbourside village of Fiskárdo, Kefalloniá

village from Vasilikí *(see p70)* to its south, or Hortáta to the north.
🔹 *Map H2 • N of Vasilikí, Lefkáda*

A stepped path in Keri, Zákynthos

Otzia, Paxí
Lying inland a little distance south of Gäios *(see p59)*, the village of Otzia is the second-largest community on the island despite its small and compact appearance. Its scenic centre is a delight – look out for the ruins of the early-Christian Church of St Marina and the little Church of St Stephen, located near the village *(see p61)*.

Travliata, Kefalloniá
Located near the pretty villages of Kástro and Lakithra *(see p84)*, with its fabulous views out to sea, Travliata is a charming village. Its traditional tavernas are very popular with visitors. The Monastery of St Andrew, with its collection of icons, lies near Travliata *(see p84)*.

Anogi, Ithaki
The scenic village of Anogi lies in the centre of the northern half of Ithaki, and is the island's most remote community. A tiny traditional collection of stone houses with gardens full of olive, cherry and cypress trees, it lies 500 m (1,600 ft) above sea level and has fabulous views of the surrounding countryside *(see p84)*.

Lagópodo, Zákynthos
One of Zákynthos's several remote mountain villages, Lagópodo is only accessed via a small road from Maherádo. If you stand in the centre of this traditional village, you will get a sense of how the islanders have lived for centuries. Established in 1962, the Eleftherotria Monastery overlooks the village. 🔹 *Map L2*
• *Near Maherádo, Zákynthos*

Keri, Zákynthos
A delightful village reached from Limni Kerious beach on the southernmost tip of Zákynthos, Keri looks out over steep cliffs to rocks and the sea beyond. It has a picturesque lighthouse and the stunning 18th-century Church of the Virgin Keriotissa, built in the Renaissance architectural style *(see p91)*.

Left **Hydropolis, Corfu** Right **Nautilus Glass Bottom Boat, Kefalloniá**

🔟 Children's Attractions

1 Aqualand, Corfu

More than 8 ha (19 acres) of countryside has been transformed into this amazing collection of water rides, giant slides and other attractions, such as the Black Hole, Kamikaze and Crazy River. Restaurants, changing rooms and relaxation areas for adults are also available. ⊗ *Map C3 • Aqualand, Corfu • 26610 58583 • Open May–Jun and Sep–Oct: 10am–6pm daily; Jul–Aug: 10am–7pm daily • Adm • www.aqualand-corfu.com*

2 Hydropolis, Corfu

Set in a large estate of landscaped gardens near Acharávi in northern Corfu, Hydropolis combines a sports and leisure centre with numerous pools, giant slides and mini versions of both for youngsters. Among its attractions are the Vortex Space Bowl and Vertigo Fall for the fearless, and water volleyball for the not-so-brave. ⊗ *Map C1 • Acharávi, Corfu • 26630 64700 • Open 10am–6:30pm daily • Adm (special rates after 4pm) • www.gelinavillage.gr*

3 Bowl'm Over, Zákynthos

With four bowling lanes, pool, foosball and air-hockey tables, and a children's play area, Bowl'm Over in Tsiliví is a great place to have some holiday fun with the family. Snacks and drinks can be enjoyed on the terrace or in the gardens. ⊗ *Map L2 • Tsiliví, Zákynthos • 26950 25142 • Open 11am–late daily • Adm • www.bowlmover.gr*

4 Luna Fun Park, Zákynthos

A children's playground with a climbing tower, bouncy castle, slides and a laser arena that resembles a war zone, complete with a World War II aeroplane, are just some of the attractions here. A babysitting service and refreshments ensure the entire family can enjoy the park. ⊗ *Map L2 • Tsiliví, Zákynthos • 26950 48035 • Open 10am–late daily • Adm • www.lunafunpark.gr*

5 Alykés Mini Golf, Zákynthos

This fun complex has greens that run through gardens and past ponds, streams, waterfalls and attractions, such as the Olympian Adventure. On-site features include cafés, a bar and beer garden, children's play area and television. ⊗ *Map L2 • Alykés, Zákynthos • 26950 83727 • Open 10am–late daily • Adm • www.alykes.com*

6 Horse and Carriage Rides, Corfu

One of the best ways to see Corfu Town is to take a horse and carriage ride, which will appeal to children of all ages. Pick-up points

A fun slide at Aqualand, Corfu

lie near the Plateia Spianáda, Palaio Frourio and Neo Frourio *(see p8)*. ◉ *Map D3 • Corfu Town, Corfu*

7 Paper Money Museum, Corfu

Children will love seeing so many banknotes together in one place in this unique museum. It explores the production process of a note, from the design to engraving and printing. The displays trace Corfu's currency down the ages, as it altered under various rulers. ◉ *Map P5 • Plateia Iroon Kypriakoú Agóna, Corfu Town, Corfu • 26610 41552 • Open 9am–1pm Tue–Thu • Adm*

8 Wildlife Walk, Corfu

This popular attraction in Corfu's north-coast resort of Sidári is ideal for the energetic or those who simply want a break from sunbathing. Families can be seen following the well-marked route, which runs alongside a river and over bridges. ◉ *Map B1 • Sidári, Corfu • 26610 37637*

9 Nautilus Glass Bottom Boat, Kefalloniá

One of many tour boats that operate out of Skála's harbour, the Nautilus follows a course to the underwater submarine wreck, the Perseus, at Mounda Bay. The trip also includes a tour of the Kakava Reef. ◉ *Map J6 • Skála, Kefalloniá • 6944 951786 • Open 10am–4pm daily • Adm*

10 Nydrí Water Sport, Lefkáda

One of the oldest attractions in Nydrí, this popular centre offers water-skiing, jet skiing, fly fishing, banana-boat rides and parasailing, which boasts fabulous coastline views. You can also take to the water in sailing boats, pedal boats or canoes. ◉ *Map J2 • Nydrí, Lefkáda • 26450 92529 • Adm • www.watersportsinlefkada.gr*

Top 10 Restaurants for Families

1 Panorama, Corfu
Family owned and run, this restaurant at Perouládes has several menu options for youngsters *(see p64)*.

2 Great Shakes, Corfu
This fun café caters to a young clientele with treats, such as chicken nuggets and mild curries *(see p66)*.

3 Agnes Restaurant, Corfu
Here children can enjoy unique Corfiot dishes made by Agnes herself *(see p48)*.

4 Taka Taka, Paxí
This restaurant has space for pushchairs and a fabulous menu of grilled fish and meat *(see p65)*.

5 Tom's Seaside Restaurant, Lefkáda
Great local dishes with salads are served at this beachside restaurant, which welcomes children *(see p74)*.

6 Trata Taverna, Lefkáda
Children love this taverna's superb food, which is cooked on a griddle. ◉ *Map J2 • Nydrí, Lefkáda • 26450 92690 • €€€*

7 The Pines, Kefalloniá
Children are sure to find a dish they like in the wide selection of meze dishes offered here *(see p88)*.

8 Pikiona, Kefalloniá
Breakfast, finger-food lunches and excellent evening meals are served at this family-friendly place *(see p88)*.

9 Mouria Restaurant, Zákynthos
Children will enjoy the tasty dishes on the extensive menu at the beachside Mouria Restaurant *(see p49)*.

10 Flocas Café, Zákynthos
A menu for young appetites makes this Argási place a family favourite *(see p99)*.

Left **Windsurfing in the Ionian Sea** Right **Snorkelling in the crystal-clear water off Corfu**

Outdoor Activities

Walking
The Ionian islands offer fabulous countryside to explore on foot. Some, such as Corfu, Ithaki and Kefalloniá, have a series of designated hiking trails that pass alongside rivers and through gorges, villages, vineyards and olive groves, as well as the odd taverna for refreshment. Always carry bottled water and a mobile phone with you.

Cycling
The terrain here is ideal for cycling, whether you prefer a leisurely ride along the coast or strenuous mountain biking. Most resorts offer bikes for hire, along with mopeds and scooters, from just a few euros a day.

Cyclists pausing for a break

Water Sports
The islands are famous for their snorkelling and diving sites, including those off Paleokastrítsa and Agios Gordios in Corfu, Lássi in Kefalloniá and Kalamáki in Zákynthos. Most resorts also have companies offering surface water sports, such as windsurfing and water-skiing. Banana-boat rides are extremely popular, especially with youngsters.

Sailing
With minimal tide variation and a mild climate, sailing around the islands is a delight. Wind speeds rarely cross 4 on the Beaufort scale in summer. The gentle *maïstro* wind blows most afternoons. Marinas and anchorages are scattered throughout the islands (see pp26–7).

Paragliding
Trailing behind a fast-moving boat on a mini-parachute is a popular activity in the Ionians, especially at large resorts, such as Nydrí in Lefkáda and Sidári in Corfu. For a small sum you can have an hour or so of exhilaration, plus great aerial coastline views.

Golf
Although there are only a handful of international-standard courses in the Ionians, golf is a popular sport here. Corfu's Ropa Valley is one of the largest complexes, with an 18-hole, par-72 course, a driving range and Pro Shop. The sport is promoted by the Hellenic Golf Federation.
🕾 21089 41933 • www.hgf.gr

Fishing off Corfu

For more information on outdoor activities See pp63, 85 and 97.

7 Tennis

Tennis has been played in Greece for centuries; in fact, it featured in the first Olympic Games in Athens in 1896. Today, most large hotels and resorts have flood-lit courts, and municipal courts are generally open to visitors. Contact the Hellenic Tennis Federation for information. ⊗ 21075 63170 • www.efoa.org.gr

8 Horse Riding

Horse rides through the countryside in the early morning or late evening, when the weather is cool, can be magical. The islands are dotted with riding clubs, such as Trailriders on Corfu and the Akrotiri Horse Riding Farm on Zakynthos. ⊗ Trailriders: www.trailriderscorfu.com • Akrotiri Horse Riding Farm: www.keomdesign.com

Riding along the coast, Kefalloniá

9 Fishing

Fishing trips are offered at many of the harbour resorts. Fish is often plentiful, and during your trip you may even spot dolphins and whales. Boats leave the harbours of the Ionians every day in the early hours of the morning.

10 Adrenaline Activities

Corfu and the Ionians offer a wide range of adrenaline sports, from gallops on horseback and sailing in strong winds to bungee jumping and thrilling water rides. Adventure-sports facilities are available at theme parks and in most resorts.

Top 10 Great Walks

1 Paleohora to Vathý, Ithaki

A 4-km (2-mile) walk from Paleohora with a break at the Melissáni cave (see p19). ⊗ Map J4

2 Kalamos to Exogi, Ithaki

A detour to the ruins of the School of Homer can be made on this 8-km (5-mile) walk. ⊗ Map H4

3 Boukari to Petriti, Corfu

Leaving Boukari, signposts lead you to Petriti on the coast. ⊗ Map D5

4 Arillas to Afionas, Corfu

This 5-km (3-mile) walk will take you past the lovely Arillas beach (see p62). ⊗ Map A2

5 Agios Stefanos to Agios Spiridhon, Corfu

This walk of 8 km (5 miles) runs along Corfu's northeast coastline. ⊗ Map D2–C1

6 Plános to Alykés, Zákynthos

This long walk on the coastal road via Psarou has sea views almost all the way. ⊗ Map L2

7 Gäios to Ballos Beach, Paxí

From Gäios, a brief walk past the sands to Ballos beach is very rewarding. ⊗ Map B5

8 Fiskárdo to Evreti, Kefalloniá

This short route along tiny lanes will give you a taste of rural life. ⊗ Map H4

9 Skála to Póros, Kefalloniá

Taking you past a light house, Akra Kapri, this walk is around 8-km (5-miles) long. ⊗ Map J6

10 Kalligoni to Lygia, Lefkáda

Challenging although short, this walk offers great views of the mainland. ⊗ Map J1

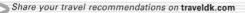

Left **Taverna Karbouris, Corfu** Right **Delfini, Lefkáda**

Restaurants

1 Agnes Restaurant, Corfu

Known for its menu of delicious home-made dishes, this charming restaurant is tucked underneath trees in the centre of Pélekas. The owner, Agnes, cooks the food herself using authentic Corfiot recipes handed down through generations. A great place to relax over a meal and watch the world go by *(see p64)*.

2 Taverna Karbouris, Corfu

Sign outside Patsouras, Kefalloniá

One of Corfu's oldest north-coast tavernas, Karbouris has become a local landmark. Traditional Greek fare, such as *kleftiko*, a lamb dish cooked in a special oven, are served here. You can sit near the swimming pool or inside in the attractive dining room *(see p64)*.

3 Tassia, Kefalloniá

Located right on Fiskárdo's harbourside, the internationally acclaimed Tassia serves great seafood dishes, pastas and salads. Its wine list is excellent, with vintages from Kefalloniá and around the world. Run by Tassia Dendrinou, a well-known cookbook author, it is a great place to relax over a good meal *(see p88)*.

4 Delfini, Lefkáda

Taverna Delfini lies on the harbourside near the pier at Vasilikí, and is a great place to watch boating activity. Always busy with both locals and visitors, it serves dishes such as *souvláki*, chargrilled steaks and fish. The ingredients are fresh and cooked to order *(see p74)*.

5 Patsouras, Kefalloniá

A taste of rural Greece in the centre of Argostóli, Patsouras serves traditional dishes that have been eaten in Kefallonián homes for generations. Dine in the courtyard on a delicious version of the local dish, *krasáto*, which is pork cooked slowly in a local wine with herbs *(see p89)*.

6 Sto Mólos, Lefkáda

If you fancy trying one of the best mezes in town then look no further than Sto Mólos, which specializes in the Greek tradition of serving several small dishes. Expect to have *kleftédes* (meatballs), *souvláki* and a host of dips, such as tzatziki and *taramosalata* brought to your table. The beer and wine here are also excellent *(see p75)*.

Sto Mólos, Lefkáda

Enjoying sweet pastries or candied fruit is the usual way to complete a meal in Greece.

7 Oinopolis Restaurant, Kefalloniá

This village restaurant offers an extensive menu of rural and international dishes, from home-made fish and meat on the spit to crepes and pasta. The wine list, which includes some Kefallonián whites and reds, is impressive. Oinopolis is full of character and a popular place to eat. ◈ Map H6
• Travliata, Kefalloniá • 26710 69988
• Open 6pm–11pm daily • €€

8 Sirines Restaurant, Ithaki

One of island's best restaurants, Sirines is run by Marina Fotopoulos, who special-izes in Ithakan cuisine. It offers international favourites as well as local dishes, such as a delicious claypot of lamb and potatoes and Ithakan tomato and feta cheese omelette. Maritime memorabilia adorns the walls. ◈ Map J4 • Ithaki Yacht Club, Vathý, Ithaki • 26740 33001
• Open 7:30pm–late daily • €€€€€

9 Zakanthi Restaurant, Zákynthos

The atmosphere of this charming restaurant in the centre of Kalamáki will have you returning time and again. Sit in the lush garden full of shrubs – it looks enchanting after dark when all the lights are lit. The tasty food, comprising mainly grills and salads, is served in generous portions (see p99).

10 Mouria Restaurant, Zákynthos

Elegant and sophisticated, the Mouria is well-known for having served excellent dishes, including seafood platters as well as desserts and fine wine, for over 50 years. This popular restaurant is located right on the beachside overlooking the Gulf of Laganás (see p92).

Top 10 Meze Dishes

1 Taramosalata
A sumptuous dip that is light pink or white in colour, taramosalata is made from cod's roe and breadcrumbs.

2 Tahini
A mixture of sesame seeds and garlic laced with lemon juice, this dip goes well with salad.

3 Kreatópita
A Kefallonián delicacy, these small pies are stuffed with a mixture of meat and local herbs.

4 Lounza
A pork loin cut, served thinly sliced and grilled with a parsley garnish, lounza often accompanies cheese.

5 Souvláki
A small kebab of diced pork or lamb on skewers, served chargrilled with lemon and herbs, souvláki is one of the most popular Greek dishes.

6 Loukanika
These small sausages, a mix of minced meat and herbs, are smoked and served with parsley.

7 Olives with Garlic
Olives are a must for every meze, but try them drenched in a mixture of olive oil and garlic.

8 Tzatziki
A refreshing dip made from natural yoghurt, diced cucumber and garlic, tzatziki goes well with just about every dish.

9 Greek Salad
Shredded cabbage and basil-covered feta are the key ingredients of a delicious Greek salad.

10 Dolmades
A distinctive Greek dish, dolmades are made by stuf-fing vine leafs with aromatic rice and ground meat.

Left **Embroidered garments for sale** Right **A range of icons**

Arts and Crafts

Lace and Embroidery
Lace is still made in many villages, as are linen items embroidered by hand. Kariá, a small village in Lefkáda, is famous for its needlecraft *(see p24)*. A local resident is said to have introduced it in the 19th century and a small museum is dedicated to the craft.

Leatherware
One of the most sought-after souvenirs for visitors to bring back from Greece is leatherware. Popular items include bags, belts and sandals, which have been made by hand in small workshops dotted around the region for centuries.

Ceramics
To get a feel for the art of creating ceramic pots, jugs and other decorative items, head off into the villages. Here locals have been making authentic products for hundreds of years. Rural ceramics tend to be unglazed rather than the colourful glazed items found in upmarket shops.

Ceramic products on display

Jewellery crafted in myriad designs

Jewellery
The tradition of wearing jewellery goes back centuries in Greece, and many modern pieces echo designs seen in ancient inscriptions. The larger towns offer a wider range of products, although rustic pieces may be found in villages. Gold and silver items are particularly good buys.

Copperware
Local communities once relied on copperware for every-day household use, but nowa-days the craft tends to be limited to making ornamental pieces only. That said, the traditional pot with a handle used to make Greek coffee is still in daily use and can be found in any good store that sells home products.

Wood Carvings
The art of carving intricate designs into wood, either as decorative plaques or into functional items, such as kitchen utensils, has been passed down through generations in Greece. Touring the gift shops on the Ionians will reveal a range of

For more information on shopping See pp67 and 86.

Spoons carved from olive wood

designs. The wood used for woodcarving is usually from local olive trees.

Rugs

The rarest of all the crafts found in the Ionians is the art of making rugs, known as *flokáti*. Made from the wool of sheep or goats and handwoven into ornate patterns, these thick rugs were used to cover the cold stone floors of village homes.

Icons

Icons depicting the Virgin and Child have been made here for centuries. The craft, although specialized, is still active today. Icons sold in gift shops are mass produced, but the ones seen in churches are genuine.

Beads

Strings of beads can be found displayed in souvenir shops throughout the region, and while many are colourful and designed as fashion accessories, others are more traditional and known as *kombolí*, or worry beads. These can be "threaded" through the fingers for relaxation.

Wall Hangings

The old craft of weaving thick cloth and mounting it on a frame is still done today. If you are lucky enough to be invited into a local home, chances are that you will see these colourful hangings adorning the walls. Shops also sell these as mementos.

Top 10 Souvenirs

1 Olive Oil
Olive oil is a speciality in the region. Bottles of olive oil, in all shapes and sizes, are available on all the islands.

2 Honey
Sweet honey has been produced for centuries in Greece and is an essential ingredient in many traditional Ionian dishes.

3 Herbs and Spices
Grown in abundance in the Ionians, an assortment of herbs and spices are dried and packaged for sale.

4 Leather Sandals
Soft leather sandals are useful and can be great reminders of a Greek holiday.

5 Plaques
Sculpted in stone, wood and resin by local artists, plaques depict scenes of rural Greece and make ideal gifts.

6 Baklava Pastries
Although unlikely to last long, these delicious honey-coated pastries are traditional souvenirs from Greece.

7 Worry Beads
Extremely addictive, worry beads are great stress-busters and hard to give up after returning home.

8 Ornate Pottery
Usually decorated with traditional designs, pottery and ceramic products, which were once essential to village life in the Ionians, make ideal holiday mementos.

9 Glyká Confectionery
Loaded with sugar but utterly divine, these candied fruits are likely to last you only until you get to the airport.

10 Embroidered Linen
An elegant reminder of the traditional attire of the Ionian islands, embroidered linen makes a lovely gift.

Corfu and the Ionians' Top 10

 Exploring a laïki agora, *or market, is a great way to find souvenirs.*

Left **Folk dancers in Skála, Kefalloniá** Right **Ochi Day parade, Corfu**

Festivals and Events

1 Litany of St Spyrídon, Corfu

The Litany of Saint Spyrídon is a religious event and music festival that takes place four times a year in Corfu. It honours Corfu's patron saint, St Spyrídon, the Keeper of the City, who is so called because of the miracle he performed in extraditing the plague from Corfu and for protecting the island from the Turkish invasion.

2 Union of the Ionians

On 21 May each year, celebrations take place throughout the islands to mark the Union of the Ionians with Greece in 1864 *(see p31)*. Cultural events, including traditional dance and music performances, are held. Whole communities gather in village centres to enjoy the entertainment and feast on local food.

3 Folklore Festivals

It is the tradition for each village in Greece to host a folklore festival at least once during the year, usually in the summer months. It is a time when residents meet up with friends and feast together. Dance troupes perform traditional dances to the accompaniment of folk bands.

4 Ochi Day

A public holiday in Greece, Ochi Day (28 October) commemorates the occasion when, in 1940, the Greek prime minister, Ioannis Metaxas, rejected an ultimatum by the Italian dictator Mussolini to allow Axis forces to occupy parts of Greece. Metaxas proclaimed *"ochi!"*, meaning "no". The event marked the beginning of Greece's involvement in World War II.

5 Litany of St Gerasímos, Kefalloniá

Kefalloniá hosts festivals for its patron saint, the 16th-century St Gerasímos *(see p37)*, on 16 August and 20 October every year. The saint, who is said to have lived the life of a hermit in a cave near Lássi, is believed to protect the people of Kefalloniá from illness.

6 Odysseus Festival, Ithaki

Ithaki, like the other islands, rarely goes a few weeks without a festival. One such event is the Odysseus Festival, held at the end of August in Vathý. The celebrations last several days and honour the legendary figures

Litany of St Gerasímos procession, Kefalloniá

of ancient Greece, King Odysseus and the poet Homer *(see p36)*, who put Ithaki on the map.

7 Cultural Festivals

Lively festivals of music, dance, theatre, art and literature are held in various towns in the Ionians during the summer months. July, for example, sees the Kefalloniá Theatre Festival, while in August, Vathý in Ithaki hosts the Music and Theatre Festival and Lefkáda hosts the Festival of Art and Literature.

8 Wine Festivals

A successful wine year is celebrated in style in the islands, with live music and feasts that are accompanied, of course, by copious amounts of local wine. Among the communities that host these events are Fragkáta in Kefalloniá, Perachóri in Ithaki, Moraitika in Corfu, Plános in Zákynthos and Lefkáda Town.

9 Town Carnivals

February or March is carnival time in the islands, when every town hosts week-long pre-Lenten events that culminate in grand processions of floats. Participants often spend weeks preparing for carnival, and people of all ages, but especially children, don interesting costumes and elaborate masks as part of the festivities.

10 International Festivals

The islands play host to several international festivals. There is the Classical Music Festival in Zákynthos, the International Folklore Festival in Lefkáda and the Argostóli International Choral Festival in Kefalloniá, to name just a few. The events are aimed at bringing together music groups from around the world.

Top 10 Drinks

1 Retsina
The traditional wine of Greece, retsina is flavoured with pine resin and can be very potent.

2 Ouzo
A strong aniseed flavoured spirit that turns milky white when water is added, ouzo is an acquired taste.

3 Greek Coffee
Greek coffee is traditionally brewed in a *briki* (a copper pot) and drunk thick and strong. Coffee in this form may take some time to appreciate, but do give it a try.

4 Metaxa
Dark brown in colour, this strong wine is matured in handmade Limousin oak casks from France and tastes rather like brandy.

5 Tsipouro
A popular and strong liquor, *tsipouro* is distilled from the residue of grapes and olives.

6 Cocktails
Colourful, usually strong and almost always highly decorated, cocktails are plentiful on the islands.

7 Kumquat Liquor
A sweet liquor flavoured with the citrus kumquat, this is a favourite on Corfu.

8 Mythos Beer
There are several good Greek beers, with Mythos being the most well known. International brews are available as well.

9 Frappé
A refreshing way to enjoy coffee, especially when the weather is hot, a frappé is a frothy cold coffee drink.

10 Soft Drinks
Most major soft-drink brands are prevalent, but try the few local versions too.

 Contact the tourist information offices for dates and timings of cultural events and festivals.

AROUND CORFU & THE IONIANS

CORFU & THE IONIANS' TOP 10

Left **Museum of Palaeopolis, Corfu** Right **Small boats moored at Pórto Longós, Paxí**

Corfu, Paxí and Antipaxí

THE LUSH ISLANDS OF CORFU, PAXÍ AND ANTIPAXÍ, *which lie between the southern tip of Italy and the western part of mainland Greece, are the* northernmost islands in the Ionian archipelago. Corfu, the second largest of the Ionians after Kefalloniá, is a curious mix of old and new. Cosmopolitan resorts, such as Benítses and Sidári, with their modern accommodation, busy bars and water-sports facilities, dot the island's pretty coastline, while traditional villages cling to the slopes of Mount Pantokrátor. The historic heart of the island's capital city, Corfu Old Town, boasts charming cobbled streets, ancient fortresses and grand palaces. The smaller islands of Paxí and Antipaxí are characterized by their natural beauty, pretty towns and bays and beaches.

Restaurants lining a street in Benítses, Corfu

🔟 Sights

1. Corfu Old Town
2. Archaeological Museum, Corfu Town
3. Mon Repos Estate, Corfu Town
4. Achílleion Palace, Corfu
5. Mount Pantokrátor, Corfu
6. Korision Lagoon, Corfu
7. Lákka, Paxí
8. Gáios, Paxí
9. Pórto Longós, Paxí
10. Antipaxí

Preceding pages **Blue Caves, Zákynthos**

1 Corfu Old Town

Inscribed as a Unesco World Heritage Site in 2007, Corfu Old Town is a remarkable blend of architectural styles. From the French-style Liston, with its chic cafés and arcaded terraces, and the Venetian buildings around the Plateía Spianáda to the imposing Palaío Frourio and Neo Frourio fortresses, the town has something for everyone. Highlights include the atmospheric Church of St Spyrídon and the oldest official building in Greece, the Palace of St Michael and St George (see pp8–9).

2 Archaeological Museum, Corfu Town

Housed in an unassuming modern building, this museum contains a fascinating collection of artifacts that explore Corfu's history. Built in the 1960s to house treasures discovered during excavation work at the ancient Temple of Artemis, in particular the famous Gorgon Medusa pediment, the museum has grown and now displays finds from other sites as well. Among them are objects unearthed from the ancient citadel in Corfu Town and from the ruins of Kassiópi's 13th-century fortress (see pp10–11).

Bustling street in Corfu Old Town

3 Mon Repos Estate, Corfu Town

Created by the second Lord High Commissioner of the Ionians, Sir Frederick Adam, this estate is famous for once being the summer home of the Greek royal family. Within its grounds are the remains of the ancient city of Palaeopolis and the palace that now houses the Museum of Palaeopolis (see pp12–13).

4 Achílleion Palace, Corfu

Located along the coast en route to Benítses, this elegant palace was the whim of Empress Elisabeth of Austria, also known as Sissi, who adored ancient Greek mythology. The palace and grounds are dotted with statues of Apollo, Hera, Achilles and Artemis. After the assassination of Elisabeth the palace remained vacant until Kaiser Wilhelm II of Germany bought it in 1907 (see pp14–15).

The main entrance hall in the Achílleion Palace, Corfu

Ferries and hydrofoils ply between Paxí's Gáios Port and Corfu's New Port on most days during summer.

Gerald Durrell

When Durrell moved with his family to Corfu as a boy in 1935, he became fascinated by the island's flora and fauna. The start of a life-long love of animals, Durrell's Corfiot years were later recounted in his Corfu Trilogy – *My Family and Other Animals* (1956), *Birds, Beasts, and Relatives* (1969) and *The Garden of the Gods* (1978).

View from atop Mount Pantokrátor, Corfu

Mount Pantokrátor, Corfu

Dominating the Corfu skyline to the north, the 900-m- (3,000-ft-) high Mount Pantokrátor is the tallest mountain on Corfu. While its south-facing slopes are carpeted with olive groves and pine forests, the slopes facing north are rugged and barren. From its peak you can see Albania and even Italy on a clear day. *Map C2*

Korisíon Lagoon, Corfu

This lagoon is home to several species of wildlife. Egrets and sandpipers, for example, can be seen around the 5-km- (3-mile-) long freshwater lake. Located on the southern coastline of Corfu, Korisíon Lagoon is separated from the Ionian Sea by a solid stretch of sand dunes and beaches, and can be reached from Mesongí. *Map D5*

Lákka, Paxí

Lákka lies to the north of the island, not far from the mysterious sea cave known as Hypapanti *(see p37)*. It is nestled in a cove that provides shelter from the strong winds of the open sea and is a popular sailing and water-sports destination. To its west are a series of excellent beaches where the sand is soft and the waters are safe for swimming. *Map A4*

Panoramic view of Lákka

8 Gáios, Paxí

Located on the eastern coastline of Paxí, the small, attractive town of Gáios is the main port and commercial centre of the island. Traditional Greek houses and tavernas line the tiny winding streets and the picturesque harbourside here. The harbour is popular with leisure sailors because the water is so calm – an offshore island, Agios Nikólaos (see p60), sits at the entrance to the harbour acting as a natural breakwater. ✎ Map B5

The waterfront at Gáios, Paxí

9 Pórto Longós, Paxí

The idyllic harbourside village of Pórto Longós lies on the east coast of Paxí, to the north of Gáios. Here, fishing and leisure boats bob in the water, tavernas selling fresh fish line the long horseshoe-shaped bay and charming houses dot the lush terraced landscape. ✎ Map B5

10 Antipaxí

Lying to the south of Paxí is the small satellite island of Antipaxí, which has a population of less than 60 permanent inhabitants. A daily boat plies to and from Paxí's Gáios harbour, although most of the islanders have their own boats and it is possible to rent one in the high season. This tiny but picturesque island is a haven of golden beaches and clear turquoise waters. ✎ Map B6

A Day Trip from Corfu Town to Paxí

Morning

🕑 Start your day by heading to Corfu Town's **New Port**. Here, look out for signs showing you where you can take the popular Flying Dolphini hydrofoil across to Paxí, which leaves at 8:30am sharp on most days during summer. Do not worry if you miss it, there is a slightly later hydrofoil departure too. Once on board you can relax in the early morning sunshine or stand on deck and enjoy the breeze. The journey time to **Gáios** in Paxí is about an hour. Once you have disembarked, you can hire a car for a few hours or take a taxi around the island. Head off north along the coastal road to the village of **Pórto Longós**, where you can explore the lively harbourside and enjoy a delicious lunch at **Nassos** (see p65), one of the excellent restaurants that line the waterfront here.

Afternoon

After lunch take the road signposted to **Lákka**. Spend some time in the the town and on nearby beaches before driving south past the tiny hamlets of **Magazia** and **Otzia** (see p61), before heading back to Gáios. While the journey is less than 10 km (6 miles), it may take a while if you stop to admire the great views. Back at Gáios, visit its Venetian square, enjoy a meal at any of the nearby restaurants, such as **Taka Taka** (see p65) or **Taverna Vassilis** (see p64), and then hop back on the hydrofoil, which departs at 7pm, for the return journey to Corfu.

➡ There are two islets at the entrance to the harbour at Gáios: Agios Nikólaos and Panagiá (Island of the Virgin Mary).

59

Left **Kassiópi, Corfu** Right **Canal d'Amour, Sidári, Corfu**

Best of the Rest

1 Ereikoússa Island

One of the three satellite islands of Corfu, together known as the Diapontian islands, Ereikoússa is characterized by its cypress trees, great beaches and the tiny yet busy town of Pórto. It is reached by boats from Sidári and Corfu Town. ◎ *Map A1*

2 Samothráki Island

The smallest Diapontian island, Samothráki is known for its quiet pace of life. Tiny communities can be found in Benatika and around the port of Plakes, where boats from Sidári arrive. ◎ *Map A1*

3 Othonoí Island

Othonoí, the largest of the Diapontians, is reached by boat from Arillas. In ancient Greek mythology, it is believed to have been the site where a shipwrecked Odysseus met Princess Nausikka, who nursed him back to health. ◎ *Map A1*

4 Gardiki Castle, Corfu

The remains of a 13th-century castle lie on Corfu's southwest coast. This Byzantine fortress was once part of the island's defenses. ◎ *Map C5 • Near Skidi village, southwest coast, Corfu*

5 Lefkimmi Town, Corfu

Divided in two – Ano Lefkimmi and Kato Lefkimmi – by a river, this wine and olive town has tall houses and tiny streets. ◎ *Map E6 • Southeast coast, Corfu*

6 Kassiópi, Corfu

The remains of a Byzantine fortification are located at this small village that has lost none of its old-world charm. It also has a pretty harbour area. ◎ *Map D1 • N of Corfu Town, Corfu*

7 Sidári, Corfu

Sidári can trace its history back to pre-Neolithic times. Today, it is a tourist resort famous for its Canal d'Amour, a natural channel cut out over millennia by the sea. Legend has it that couples who swim through this "Canal of Love" will stay together forever. ◎ *Map B1 • Ormos Sidári, Corfu*

8 Benítses, Corfu

One of the liveliest tourist attractions on the island, this east-coast resort has tavernas and nightspots and offers endless water sports. ◎ *Map D4 • S of Corfu Town, Corfu*

9 Agios Nikólaos Islet, Paxí

Lying in the entrance to Gäios on Paxí, Agios Nikólaos has two churches and a fort believed to be Byzantine. ◎ *Map B5 • Off Gäios New Port, Paxí*

10 Panagiá Islet, Paxí

Panagiá islet, or the Island of the Virgin Mary, also lies at the entrance to Gäios. Its hilltop basilica, dedicated to the Virgin, and its rugged shoreline are best seen from the deck of a boat. ◎ *Map B5 • Off Gäios New Port, Paxí*

Ereikoússa, Samothráki and Othonoí make up the Diapontian islands, situated off the northwest coast of Corfu.

Left **Pélekas, Corfu** Right **Kalámi, Corfu**

🔟 Picturesque Villages

1 Kávos, Corfu
While Kávos is usually considered a haunt of the young and trendy, the heart of the village is more traditional. Do not let the bright lights detract you from its scenic beauty. ◈ *Map F6*

2 Pélekas, Corfu
This pretty hamlet offers not only great beaches and tavernas, but also a real sense of community, village folklore and a rich cultural heritage. It is easily reached from Corfu Town. ◈ *Map C4 • W of Corfu Town, Corfu*

3 Agios Markos, Corfu
Resting at the foothills of Mount Pantokrátor, this village lies along the road from Barbati to Ano Korakiana. Its picturesque Heptanesian architecture is particularly noteworthy. ◈ *Map C2 • East coast, Corfu*

4 Barbati, Corfu
Although known more for its exquisite and unspoilt 2-km- (1-mile-) long beach, complete with the remains of an ancient church in the shingle, this is one of Corfu's prettiest east-coast villages. ◈ *Map C2 • East coast, Corfu*

5 Vátos, Corfu
The charming village of Vátos is made up of tiny streets and bougainvillea-covered stone houses that have stood for decades. It looks out over the west coast beaches of Myrtiótissa and Ermones. ◈ *Map B3 • West Corfu*

6 Kalámi, Corfu
Set in a horseshoe-shaped bay, this traditional village was once home to the British author Lawrence Durrell (1912–1990). Its pebble beach boasts the prestigious Blue Flag Award. ◈ *Map D2 • Northeast coast, Corfu*

7 Krini, Corfu
Known for its beautiful location and fabulous sea views, Krini is a traditional village that oozes charm. Near it lies the Byzantine Angelokastro fortress. ◈ *Map A2 • West coast, Corfu*

8 Gouvia, Corfu
Located on the site of a Venetian harbour and home to Corfu's largest marina (see p26), Gouvia is a delightful village with a cosmopolitan edge. Its traditional stone buildings house chic tavernas. ◈ *Map C3 • East coast, Corfu*

9 Otzia, Paxí
Paxí's second-largest community after Gäios, Otzia is the most southerly village on the island. Its harbour has huge boulders through which wind holes have been eroded, while nearby are the ruins of an ancient church (see p43). ◈ *Map B5*

10 Magazia, Paxí
Close to the Stachai caves and, a little further on, the Petriti cave, Magazia is probably best known for its fabulous sunsets. This traditional village lies inland amid olive groves. ◈ *Map A5*

The Blue Flag award, won by Corfu's Kalámi beach, recognizes sustainable development of beaches around the world.

Left **Arillas beach, Corfu** Right **Voutoumi beach, Antipaxí**

Bays and Beaches

Arillas Beach, Corfu
Tucked into Corfu's northwest corner, Arillas is a long and sandy stretch of beautiful beach. You can watch the sea break on the islets that lie just off the shoreline.
⊗ Map A2 • Near Agios Stefanos, Corfu

Yaliskari Beach, Corfu
Head for this tranquil beach, tucked away in a small cove, if you want a truly peaceful holiday. This off-the-beaten-track gem is only accessible from Sinarades and few people take the small winding road down from the town. ⊗ Map C4 • Near Pélekas, Corfu

Myrtiótissa Beach, Corfu
Described as Europe's most stunning beach, this horseshoe-shaped beach lives up to its reputation. With no tavernas and only sheer cliffs and golden sands, it is a favourite with nature-lovers. ⊗ Map B4 • West coast, Corfu

Paleokastrítsa Beach, Corfu
Sheltered by a cove, this popular beach is famous for being Sir Frederick Adams' (see p13) favourite. Tavernas provide shade and refreshments. ⊗ Map B3 • Ormos Liapádhon, west coast, Corfu

Agrilas Bay, Paxí
Lying north of Otzia, this bay is one of the largest sweeps of rugged coastline on the west coast. It has a few tiny beaches, including the pretty Avlaki beach. ⊗ Map A5 • West coast, Paxí

Soulalenia Beach, Paxí
Located on the outskirts of Gäios, Soulalenia beach is one of several popular beaches along this stretch of coastline. Others include Yanna and Kaki Langada, which is surrounded by rocks.
⊗ Map B5 • Near Gäios, Paxí

Arkoudaki Beach, Paxí
Accessible only by boat, the small and beautifully secluded Arkoudaki beach is located on the northeastern tip of Paxí. It is a favourite spot for sailors to jump off their yachts. ⊗ Map A4 • Near Lákka, Paxí

Levechio Beach, Paxí
This attractive beach lies a little way south of Pórto Longós. It is largely made up of fine shingle, and attracts many visitors in the summer months.
⊗ Map B5 • East coast, Paxí

Vrika Beach, Antipaxí
Antipaxí is known for its fabulous golden sandy beaches, and Vrika is probably the most famous of these. The journey there takes you through a country-side of vineyards. ⊗ Map B6

Voutoumi Beach, Antipaxí
Lying just north of Vrika is Voutoumi, the other well-known beach on Antipaxí. It is popular due to its turquoise seas and an attractive stretch of sand and pebbles. A walkway links it to Vrika beach. ⊗ Map B6 • S of Vrika beach, Paxí

For more beaches in Corfu and Antipaxí **See pp32–3.**

Left **Sailing** Right **Ermones Golf Club, Corfu**

Outdoor Activities

Nature Trails
All the islands have nature trails, but Antipaxí is particularly popular with nature-lovers as it is relatively small and easy to navigate. Its countryside boasts a wealth of wildlife, such as weasels, foxes and hedgehogs.

Sailing
The bays, beaches and coves of Corfu, Paxí and Antipaxí are a delight to explore on a sailing boat. The islands all have harbours where leisure boats can moor. Corfu also boasts the fabulous Gouvia Marina *(see p26)*.

Swimming
While some bays are protected, others have strong currents and swimmers should take care. Gently sloping beaches for safe offshore swimming include those at Benítses *(see p60)* on Corfu and near Gäios *(see p59)* on Paxí.

Beachcombing
The beaches on the islands offer numerous opportunities for beachcombing for items washed ashore, such as driftwood and seashells. Always respect the environment and do not litter the beach.

Archaeological Tours
The tourist office in Corfu Town can provide information on specialist companies offering archaeological tours. Organized trips to interesting archaeological destinations include tours to Mon Repos *(see p12–13)* on Corfu and Hypapanti *(see p37)* on Paxí.

Cycling
All the major tourist resorts have companies offering bicycles for hire. However, unless you are particularly athletic and like rough terrain, it is best to stay on the level ground around the towns.

Golf
Corfu's 18-hole, 72-par Rópa Valley and Ermones courses are two of a handful of international-standard courses in the Ionians. Less challenging mini versions are found at the resorts.

Horse Riding
While horse riding is not a major activity on Corfu or Paxí, a few schools, including Trailriders *(see p47)* near Mount Pantokrátor on Corfu, offer rides into the olive grove-scattered countryside.

Water Sports
Major resorts offer plenty of water sports, from scuba diving, water-skiing and windsurfing to banana-boat rides, canoeing and pedalo rides. The resorts that offer training as well are Corfu's Sidári, Benítses and Kassiópi *(see p60)*.

Walking
If you like walking in the open countryside, then the islands will give you every opportunity for walks along coastal roads or in the rugged inland terrain.

Left **Janis Restaurant, Corfu** Right **Taverna Vassilis, Paxí**

TOP 10 Traditional Tavernas

1 Agnes Restaurant, Corfu
This delightful restaurant has a reputation for good, wholesome dishes prepared by the owner, Ágnes, using only organic ingredients. ⬡ *Map C4 • Pélekas, Corfu • 26610 94997 • Open 8am–late daily • €€€€*

2 Taverna Karbouris, Corfu
Set in the charming village of Néa Períthia, Karbouris uses traditional Corfiot recipes that have been handed down through the generations. ⬡ *Map C1 • Agios Spyrídon, Néa Períthia, Corfu • 26630 98032 • Open 9:30am–11pm daily • €€€*

3 Vergina, Corfu
This traditional taverna, housed in a former bakery, serves local favourites, such as *souvláki*. There is also Greek music and dancing here.
⬡ *Map C3 • Gouvia, Corfu • 26610 90093 • Open 9am–late daily • €€€*

4 Panorama, Corfu
Perched high on a cliff on the coast near Sidári, this atmospheric eatery boasts fantastic sunset views. Meat grills and local fare are served here.
⬡ *Map A1 • Perouládes, Corfu • 26630 95035 • Open 10am–late daily • €€€*

5 Taverna Sebastian, Corfu
Established in 1977, Taverna Sebastian specializes in traditional Corfiot dishes inspired by the staff's own recipes. ⬡ *Map C4 • Agios Gordios, Sinarades, Corfu • 26610 53256 • €€€*

6 Janis Restaurant, Corfu
With alfresco dining terraces overlooking Kalamionas Bay, and a good Greek menu, this restaurant has quite a following. It is best to book ahead. ⬡ *Map D1 • Kassiópi, Corfu • 26630 81082 • Open 11am–late daily • €€€*

7 Chrisi Tavern, Corfu
This popular tavern was established in the 1920s. Its signature dish is *sofrito*, a Venetian meal of meat in a garlic and white-wine sauce. ⬡ *Map D3 • Corfu Town, Corfu • 26610 46175 • Open 11am–1pm daily*

8 Toula's Seafood Restaurant, Corfu
Toula uses fresh ingredients, such as tomato, lemon and garlic, to create traditional Corfiot seafood dishes with a modern twist.
⬡ *Map D2 • Agni Bay, Corfu • 26630 91350 • Open 12:30pm–11pm daily • €€€€*

9 Rex, Corfu
Serving Corfiot dishes, such as *bakaliaropitta*, a light stuffed pastry, this landmark restaurant is housed in a 19th-century building. ⬡ *Map P5 • Kapodistriou 66, Corfu Town, Corfu • 26610 39649 • Open 11am–late daily • €€€€*

10 Taverna Vassilis, Paxí
One of Gäios's many traditional tavernas, Vassilis offers dishes such as octopus in red wine, *souvláki* and grills. ⬡ *Map B5 • Main square, Gäios, Paxí • 26620 30062 • Open 11am–late daily • €€€€*

Above **Trilogia Restaurant, Corfu**

Price Categories

For a three-course meal for one with half a bottle of wine (or equivalent meal), taxes and extra charges.

€ under €20
€€ €20–€30
€€€ €30–€40
€€€€ €40–€50
€€€€€ over €50

🔟 Restaurants

1 Lemon Garden Restaurant, Corfu

A barbecue restaurant serving tasty chicken, steak and fish cooked with herbs and sauces, as well as delicious *souvláki*, Lemon Garden is popular with locals. Wine comes from the owner's vineyard. ✆ Map C1
• Acharávi, Corfu • 26630 64446 • Open 11am–late daily • €€€€

2 Bistro Boileau, Corfu

At this stylish bistro, age-old Greek recipes are given a refreshing contemporary twist. The local wines on offer here complement the food. ✆ Map C3
• Kontokáli, Corfu • 26610 90069 • Open summer: 7pm–late Sun–Sat; winter: 6pm–late Tue–Sat • €€€€€

3 Trilogia Restaurant, Corfu

Overlooking the sea at Kassiópi, Trilogia offers à la carte dishes with a Corfiot twist. The wine list is excellent. ✆ Map D1
• Seafront Kassiópi, Corfu • 26630 81589 • Open 10am–late daily • €€€€€

4 Ninos on the Beach Restaurant, Corfu

Serving traditional Corfiot dishes and local wines, Ninos offers panoramic views of the bay. ✆ Map C1
• Kristi, near Acharávi, Corfu • 26630 63291 • Open 8am–late daily • €€€

5 EY Lounge Café, Corfu

A chic, bistro-style café that offers light European-inspired dishes, including pasta and salad, the EY Lounge Café is an ideal spot for lunch. ✆ Map P5
• Kapodistiou, Corfu Town, Corfu • 26610 80670 • Open 11am–11pm daily • €€€

6 La Famiglia, Corfu

The elegant La Famiglia celebrates all things Italian with authentic dishes and wines from Italy. ✆ Map P5 • Maniarizi Artiovti 16, Corfu Town, Corfu • 26610 30270 • Open 8pm–11:30pm daily • €€€€€

7 Rouvas Restaurant, Corfu

This cosy place uses local produce and serves Greek dishes, such as *kleftiko*, a tender lamb stew. ✆ Map P3 • Stamatiou Desylia 13, Corfu Town, Corfu • 26610 31182 • Open 10am–5pm daily • €€€

8 Taka Taka, Paxí

The landmark Taka Taka serves great barbecued meat and fish dishes on its vine-covered terrace. Its wine list showcases local vineyards. ✆ Map B5 • Gáios, Paxí • 26620 32329 • Open 10am–late daily • €€€

9 Nassos, Paxí

This eatery serves dishes that capture the true experience of Paxí, from swordfish to octopus in delicate sauces. ✆ Map B5
• Harbour, Pórto Longós, Paxí • 26620 31604 • Open 8am–late daily • €€€€

10 Karkaletzos Tavern, Paxí

This tavern offers real Greek dishes, such as *bourthéto*, a spicy fish stew, and grills. ✆ Map B5
• Makratika, Gáios, Paxí • 26620 32129 • Open 10am–late daily• €€€

Left **Akron Beach Bar, Corfu** Right **Capriccio Café, Paxí**

TOP 10 Cafés, Bars and Clubs

1 Central, Corfu
By day this chic café serves healthy breakfasts and light lunches, and by night is transformed into a hip cocktail bar. ✆ *Map C1 • Acharávi, Corfu • 26630 63204 • Open 8am–late daily*

2 Harbour Bar, Corfu
Relax over morning coffee or evening drinks at this bar, located at the water's edge at Kassiópi. ✆ *Map D1 • The harbour, Kassiópi, Corfu • 26630 81227 • Open 8am–late daily*

3 Palazzo Cocktail Bar, Corfu
This lively bar located on Sidári's main thoroughfare serves snacks from early morning through the afternoon and evening, when elaborate cocktails are also on offer. The food served here is international. ✆ *Map B1 • Sidári, Corfu • 26630 95946 • Open 8am–late daily*

4 La Grótta, Corfu
Be sure to visit this vibrant, subtly lit bar housed underground in a cave off the beach. Enjoy the cocktails and light snacks here. ✆ *Map B3 • Paleokastrítsa, Corfu • 26630 41006 • Open 10am–late daily*

5 Stagousta Club, Corfu
Decor inspired by Greek mythology, colourful cocktails, live music, and a young and trendy clientele that enjoys dancing till dawn have put this club on the map. ✆ *Map C4 • Agios Gordios, Corfu • 26610 53924*

6 7th Heaven Café, Corfu
Enjoy drinks and grills while taking in the sunset at this west-coast café overlooking Logas beach. It is affiliated to the Panorama restaurant *(see p64)*.

7 Great Shakes, Corfu
With bright decor and a palm-surrounded outdoor terrace, this is one of the oldest and liveliest cafés in Dasía. The menu has classics, such as scampi and chips, and curries. ✆ *Map C3 • Dasía, Corfu • 26610 93789 • Open 7–10:30pm daily*

8 Akron Beach Bar, Corfu
The popular Akron Beach Bar offers freshly made fruit juices, cocktails and soft drinks. Its restaurant serves salads and snacks. ✆ *Map B3 • Paleokastrítsa, Corfu • 26630 41226 • Open summer: 9:30am–sunset*

9 Angelos Bar, Corfu
Satellite screens showing sport and news channels, comfortable seating, cosy decor and music from the 1960s to the 80s ensure that the Angelos Bar at Kassiópi is always lively. ✆ *Map D1 • Kassiópi, Corfu • 26630 81022 • Open 11am–late daily*

10 Capriccio Café, Paxí
Delicious-looking pastries, cakes and several flavours of ice cream are some of the delights offered at this café. ✆ *Map B5 • Gäios, Paxí • 26620 32687 • Open 11am–6pm daily*

ivy-covered tavernas serving fresh seafood. There is a beach here as well. ✎ *Map J3 • Ormos Syvota, Lefkáda*

Cavo Nira

Lying on the island's south coast, Cavo Nira overlooks the bay of Vasilikí and the Lipsopirgos peninsula. This area is known as the site where, according to Greek mythology, the god Apollo was worshipped. Nearby are the remains of a sanctuary, marked today by the church of St Nikólaos Niras. On this stretch of coast-line are the cliffs from where the poet Sappho *(see p36)* is believed to have jumped to her death, after being rejected by her conceited lover, Phaon. ✎ *Map H3 • Lipsopirgos peninsula, Lefkáda*

Pórto Katsiki Beach

Widely considered to be one of the best beaches in Greece, if not Europe, Pórto Katsiki lies on the west coast of the large peninsula that leads to Cape Lefkáda *(see p72)*, which is located to the south of the island. Its striking white cliffs, topped by lush vegetation, drop vertically to the golden sand below, which is lapped by a brilliant turquoise sea. This beach can be reached via a small road from Athani, via the village of Melios, or on a boat from Nydrí or Vasilikí. Facilities are few but it is a great place to relax. ✎ *Map H3 • Near Cape Lefkáda, Lefkáda*

The pristine Pórto Katsiki beach

A Morning on the East Coast

🕐 Start your day in **Lefkáda Town** and take the coast road, following signs to **Lygia**. Stop when you reach this fishing village – visit its bustling harbour and enjoy the peace and quiet. Next head for **Nikiana** and see the much larger harbour here, before heading off to the beautiful **Perigialia** resort *(see p72)* and then on to Nydrí.

☕ Stop for coffee at **Nydrí**. Here you can choose any one of the several tavernas that line the harbourside and enjoy the sight of yachts and fishing boats passing by the waterfront. Look across to the islands of **Skorpidi**, **Sparti** and **Madouri** *(see p72)* to the east. Before setting off again to explore the island further south, follow the signs to the **Nydrí water-falls**, which are worth the detour. Cool off under the spray from the cataracts.

Back on the road, head south along the coast past **Vlycho**. From here the road leads inland to a small village, where you will reach a fork. If you take the road to your left you can visit **Póros** *(see p72)* and **Mykros Yalos** *(see p73)*, while the road to the right heads off to Vasilikí via a couple of small villages. After you arrive at **Vasilikí** you can stop for a leisurely lunch overlooking the bay. You may find it a bit breezy here – windsurfers are likely to be out enjoying their sport. For your return trip, retrace your route along the coastal road or alternatively take the mountain road signposted to Lefkáda Town.

Left **Póros village** Right **A house in the mountain village of Sivros**

Best of the Rest

1 Meganísi Island
Life on Meganísi, the largest island off Lefkáda, revolves around its capital, the village of Váthy, with its lovely waterfront tavernas offering delicious local cuisine. ❧ Map J2 • W of Póros, Lefkáda

2 Madouri Island
This small island, covered in vegetation, is tucked into the bay off Nydrí, sandwiched between the town and the island of Sparti. It is easily accessed by boat. ❧ Map J2 • NW of Nydrí, Lefkáda

3 Sparti Island
Sparti is the most northerly of the huddle of islands that lie off the east coast of Lefkáda. It is characterized by dense under-growth that extends to its coastline. ❧ Map J2 • NW of Nydrí, east coast, Lefkáda

4 Skorpidi Island
This is one of the smallest islands lying off Lefkáda's coast. Its unspoilt countryside and coastline offer excellent opportunities for exploration. You can take a boat across from Nydrí for a relaxing day trip. ❧ Map J2 • W of Nydrí, Lefkáda

5 Perigialia
Best known for its 15th-century church where, in the 19th century, revolutionaries hid against the British Protectorate, Pergialia is now a popular haunt of visitors keen to experience village life. ❧ Map J2 • Near Nydrí, Lefkáda

6 Póros
With its tiny alleyways and bougainvillea-covered stone houses, Póros is a must on any holiday itinerary. The Church of Analipsi here has some notable 16th-century icons, and there are the ruins of a fortress nearby. ❧ Map J2 • Ormos Rouda, Lefkáda

7 Kariá
Often known as Karyá, this pretty mountain village lies in central Lefkadá and has managed to retain its traditional way of life. The popular craft of intricate embroidery continues to flourish here. ❧ Map H2

8 Cape Lefkáda
Although bleak and barren, this peninsula, the island's southernmost point, is enchanting, with its sheer cliffs that contrast sharply with the blue of the sea. It is reached by a tiny, uneven road. ❧ Map H3

9 Sivros
Lying in the heart of Lefkadá is the remote mountain village of Sivros – a cluster of stone houses surrounded by laurel woods. It has very few modern amenities. ❧ Map H2 • N of Vasilikí, Lefkáda

10 Agios Nikitas
A short drive from Lefkáda Town takes you to this small fishing village, which has been transformed into one of the island's prettiest and most chic resorts. ❧ Map H1 • SW of Lefkáda Town, Lefkáda

Left **Picturesque Kathísma beach** Right **Tranquil Póros beach**

🔟 Beaches

1 Mýlos Beach
This scenic beach is famous for its iconic 18th-century stone windmill, which would not look out of place on a postcard. Today, the building functions as a café. Steps lead down to the soft sandy beach *(see p25)*.

2 Mykros Yalos Beach
Lying in the Ormos Rouda bay, just south of Póros, is the pebble beach of Mykros Yalos. It is a preferred summer holiday destination. ✆ *Map J2 • Ormos Rouda, Lefkáda*

3 Egremini Beach
Not to be confused with a smaller beach of the same name located near Agios Nikitas, the stunning Egremini beach lies close to Athani village. It can be accessed only by a tiny unpaved road. ✆ *Map H2 • Athani, Lefkáda*

4 Pefkoulia Beach
This popular beach is a large sweep of sand on the west coast near Agios Nikitas. The turquoise water boasts ideal swimming conditions. ✆ *Map H1 • N of Agios Nikitas, Lefkáda*

5 Kathísma Beach
Lying near the village of Kalamítsi, Kathísma beach is long and wide and boasts soft-white sand. With some interesting caves and rocks for exploration, this beach has become one of the most visited on Lefkáda. ✆ *Map H2 • Kalamítsi, Lefkáda*

6 Nikiana Beach
Found not far from the village of Nikiana, this beach is one of the sandiest in the area. Tavernas and bars have steadily appeared, making it popular with holiday-makers. ✆ *Map J2 • Nikiana, Lefkáda*

7 Póros Beach
Not far from Mykros Gialos, Póros beach lies south of the town of the same name. It is quieter than its neighbour, Mykros Gialos, and is favoured by visitors who like camping. ✆ *Map J2 • Ormos Rouda, Lefkáda*

8 Vasilikí Beach
Vasilikí beach is best known for its excellent sailing and wind-surfing conditions. Dedicated clubs provide both instruction and equipment. It has facilities such as tavernas and bars. ✆ *Map H3 • Ormos Vasilikís, Lefkáda*

9 Gialos Beach
This shingle beach can be reached via a sharply descending, winding road followed by a series of tracks. Its tranquil feel makes the journey worthwhile. ✆ *Map H2 • Athani, Lefkáda*

10 Megalo Limonari Beach
Remote and beautiful, Megalo Limonari beach on the island of Meganísi can be accessed from Katomerí village on Meganísi's south coast. Sandy and surrounded by trees, it sits in an attractive bay. ✆ *Map J2 • Near Katomerí, Meganísi*

Left **Tom's Seaside Restaurant, Nydrí** Right **The interior of Delfini, Vasilikí**

TOP10 Restaurants

1 Tom's Seaside Restaurant
This popular restaurant lies in lush gardens and has a menu of local dishes, such as moussaka, *souvláki* and beautifully presented lobster. ◎ *Map J2 • Nydrí, Lefkáda • 26450 92928 • Open noon–late daily • €€*

2 Delfini
Located near the pier at Vasilikí, this taverna serves chargrilled fish and steaks, plus local dishes, such as *souvláki*. ◎ *Map H2 • Harbourside, Vasilikí, Lefkáda • 26450 31430 • Open all day • €€€*

3 Tropicana Restaurant
Known for its home-made pizzas and chargrilled *souvláki*, Tropicana lies in Spartochóri's village centre and has views out towards Lefkáda. ◎ *Map J2 • Spartochóri, Meganísi island • 26450 51486 • Open noon–late daily • €*

4 Apóllon Restaurant
Located inside the Apóllon Hotel *(see p112)*, this attractive eatery, with views of the Ormos Vasilikis bay, is open to non-residents. It serves a delicious buffet-style breakfast and à la carte evening meals.

5 Olive Tree Restaurant
This atmospheric family-run establishment, set within an olive grove, has been around for over 20 years. Recipes used here have been handed down through the generations. ◎ *Map J2 • Nydrí, Lefkáda • 26450 92655 • Open 6pm–late daily • €€*

6 Sapfo Hall, Ionian Star
Located in the Ionian Star Hotel, the bright and airy Sapfo Hall serves international cuisine. Eat indoors or take advantage of the veranda, with its panoramic harbour views. ◎ *Map J1 • Harbour, Lefkáda Town, Lefkáda • 26450 24762 • Open 7am–late daily • €€*

7 Lefkáda Beach Restaurant
Set in the heart of Lygia village, this restaurant specializes in breakfasts and light snacks and offers excellent views of the harbour. ◎ *Map J1 • Lygia, Lefkáda • 26450 72216 • Open 7am–2pm daily • €€*

8 Sapfo Restaurant
The Sapfo, which is located right next to the beach at Agios Nikitas, serves international and local favourites such as steak and grilled fish. ◎ *Map H1 • Agios Nikitas beach, Lefkáda • 26450 97497 • Open noon–late daily • €€*

9 Minas
Known for its dishes of fresh fish caught by its own fishing crew and served with herbs from its garden, this attractive restaurant lies overlooking the bay. ◎ *Map J2 • Nikiana, Lefkáda • 26450 71192 • Open 11am–late daily • €€€*

10 The Barrel
A good mix of international dishes complemented by Greek cuisine is served at this open-air restaurant at the marina. ◎ *Map J2 • Nydrí Marina, Nydrí, Lefkada • 26450 92906 • Open noon–late daily • €€€*

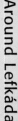

Price Categories

For a three-course meal for one with half a bottle of wine (or equivalent meal), taxes and extra charges.

€ under €20
€€ €20–€30
€€€ €30–€40
€€€€ €40–€50
€€€€€ over €50

Above **Regantos, Lefkáda Town**

⑩ Traditional Tavernas

Sto Mólos
Delicious *souvláki* and dips are served here in an endless stream of mezes with local wine and beer from the cask. ◎ *Map J1 • Golemi, Lefkáda Town, Lefkáda • 26450 24879 • Open noon–late daily • €€*

Limni Taverna
Standing in lavish gardens, Limni serves traditional Greek fare, such as barbecued fish and a typical Peloponnesian lamb dish. ◎ *Map J1 • Eptanese, Lygia, Lefkáda • 26450 71540 • Open noon–late daily • €€*

Café Liotrivi
Overlooking Ormos Syvota bay, this atmospheric café is housed in a former olive-oil press. Old equipment lines its walls, with the olive press forming the centerpiece. It offers light snacks. ◎ *Map J3 • Syvota, Lefkáda • 26450 31870 • Open 11am–late daily • €€*

O Molos
Home-made dishes, such as moussaka and fresh seafood platters, are the specialties at this restaurant. Watch the world go by from its terrace. ◎ *Map J2 • Harbour, Mykros Yalos, Lefkáda • 26450 95548 • Open 8pm–late daily • €€€*

Regantos
Chargrilled fish dishes served with a creative flair are the order of the day at this popular town-centre restaurant. Sip home-made wine on the terrace. ◎ *Map J1 • Lefkáda Town, Lefkáda • 26450 22855 • Open 7:30pm–late daily • €€€€€*

Keramidaki Taverna
Mature olive trees give the terrace here its charm and provide welcome shade from the sun. The menu features superb herb-infused seafood. ◎ *Map J2 • Nikiana, Lefkáda • 26450 92417 • Open 1pm–late daily • €€€*

Taverna Riviera
Located next to a park, this taverna serves meze, grills and Greek dishes, such as *kleftédes*, with local wines. ◎ *Map J1 • Harbour, Lefkada Town, Lefkáda • 26450 21480 • Open 10am–late daily • €€€*

Taverna Oasis
Surrounded by huge trees, the Oasis serves goat, rabbit and other meats straight off the coals. ◎ *Map H3 • Pórto Katsiki, Lefkáda • 26450 33201 • Open 11am–late daily • €€*

Laki's Taverna
The bougainvillea-covered Laki's Taverna is on one of the many cobbled alleyways found in the village of Spartochóri on Meganísi island. It serves home-made local dishes. ◎ *Map J2 • Spartochóri, Meganísi island • 26450 51228 • Open 7pm–late daily • €€€*

Taverna Karaboulis
Located in Kariá, a traditional mountain village that is a favourite with visitors for its intricate embroidery, Taverna Karaboulis serves delicious local dishes with a modern twist. ◎ *Map H2 • Kariá, Lefkáda • 26450 413010 • Open 11am–late daily • €€€*

Left **The attractive port at Sámi, Kefalloniá** Right **Waterfront houses in Vathý, Ithaki**

Kefalloniá and Ithaki

B EAUTIFUL, RUGGED AND DENSELY FORESTED KEFALLONIÁ, *with its 250-km- (160-mile-) long coastline, is the largest island in the Ionians and the sixth-largest in Greece. Dominating the island is Mount Eros (Aínos), which, at 1,600 m (5,200 ft) above sea level, is the highest peak in the archipelago. Elsewhere, dramatic scenery can be found in every corner of the island. Subterranean waterways, deep caves, pebbly beaches, wild mountain slopes and natural springs are all part of its geological make-up. Neighbouring*

Ithaki lies to the northeast of Kefalloniá's main port, Sámi. This unspoilt idyll is widely considered to have been the homeland of legendary King Odysseus. Like its bigger sister to the west, Ithaki is thought to have been inhabited since prehistoric times.

Agrostóli harbourside, Kefalloniá

🔟 Sights

1. Mýrtou Bay, Kefalloniá
2. Sámi, Kefalloniá
3. Caves of Sámi, Kefalloniá
4. Argostóli, Kefalloniá
5. Fiskárdo, Kefalloniá
6. Palaiokastró, Kefalloniá
7. Skála, Kefalloniá
8. Asos, Kefalloniá
9. Vathý, Ithaki
10. Piso Aetós, Ithaki

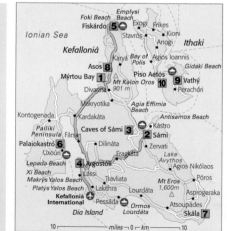

Preceding pages **Stunning Navagio beach, Zákynthos**

1 Mýrtou Bay, Kefaloniá

With its brilliant turquoise sea, horseshoe-shaped white beach and backdrop of huge cliffs, Mýrtou Bay on Kefallonia's west coast is widely considered to be one of the most beautiful in the world. The picture-postcard bay is flanked by the mountains of Agia Dynati and Kalon Oros. The bay can be reached via a steeply descending road from Divarata village (see pp16–17).

Spectacular Mýrtou Bay, Kefaloniá

2 Sámi, Kefaloniá

Sámi, which lies northeast of the capital, Argostóli, on the island's east coast, is Kefaloniá's principal port. This attractive town boasts traditional-style buildings overlooking the bay, where ferries and boats provide a constant source of fascination. A popular tourist hotspot, Sámi offers a good choice of restaurants and bars. Popular sights include the pebbly beach of Antisamos (see p83), nearby Karavomylos and the area's many caves.
§ Map H5 • East coast, Kefallonia

3 Caves of Sámi, Kefaloniá

Drogkaráti cave is a wonder of nature. Believed to be more than a million years old, this massive space was discovered more than 300 years ago when an earthquake revealed its entrance. Extraordinary stalactites and stalagmites can be spotted by visitors on their way to the Royal Balcony, a natural rock platform, and the Chamber of Exaltation, a popular operatic concert venue. Other caves include Angalaki, the largest in the area, and Melissáni, with its famous subterranean waterway where artifacts dating from the 4th century BC have been discovered (see pp18–19).

4 Argostóli, Kefaloniá

A charming town lying in a large bay, Argostóli is the capital of Kefaloniá. Life here revolves around the central square, Plateia Valliánou. Always a hive of activity, it is here that visitors can find great restaurants and superlative shopping along the Lithóstroto. Argostóli was almost entirely destroyed in the 1953 earthquake, but has since been rebuilt in keeping with its former architectural style. The Historical and Folk Museum located here has a superb collection of photographs depicting the destruction and rebuilding of the town.
§ Map G5 • Historical and Folk Museum: Ilía Zervoú 12 • 26710 28835 • Open Feb–Nov: 9am–2pm Mon–Sat • Adm

A busy street in Argostóli, Kefaloniá

Earthquakes in the Ionians

The Ionians lie on a major geological fault, where the European and Aegean tectonic plates meet. Tension between the plates creates ongoing seismic activity; this is usually minor, but a few times each century, earthquakes occur. The largest in recent years, at 7.3 on the Richter scale, was on 12 August 1953. Its epicentre lay just off Kefalloniá.

Fiskárdo, Kefalloniá

5 Fiskárdo, Kefalloniá

Fiskárdo is the only village in Kefalloniá to have escaped damage in the 1953 earthquake. Original pastel-coloured Venetian buildings line the pretty harbourside here, and a busy marina and ferry dock as well as seafood restaurants, tavernas and bars ensure its popularity with locals and visitors alike. It is surrounded by a landscape clothed in cypress trees, and offers wonderful views of its neighbour, Ithaki. ⊗ Map H4 • North coast, Kefalloniá

6 Palaiokastró, Kefalloniá

Palaiokastró is believed to be one of the oldest sites in the Ionians. A series of archaeological excavations were conducted here some years ago after the discovery of ancient remains. Further ruins of walls, possibly belonging to ancient houses, and a fortress that may have once formed part of a city, were unearthed. Nearby are tombs that have been dated to around 1600 BC, when the ancient Mycenaean civilization ruled Kefalloniá. ⊗ Map G5 • Pallikí peninsula, Kefalloniá

7 Skála, Kefalloniá

An attractive town on the southeastern tip of the island, Skála offers a good choice of sandy beaches, restaurants, hotels, attractions for children, shops and nightlife. The earthquake of 1953 destroyed much of the town's original architecture, the remains of which can still be seen. A little out of town are beautiful pine forests, and further inland you will find the Roman Villa (see p37), an archaeological site with some well-preserved mosaics that once adorned the floor of an impressive mansion. ⊗ Map J6 • Southeast coast, Kefalloniá

8 Asos, Kefalloniá

An unspoilt village near Mýrtou Bay, Asos can be reached by a sharply descending road that winds down from a high stone terraced hillside to the sea. It lies in a small harbour and is characterized by charming traditional architecture. A strip of land

Beautiful Asos from above, Kefalloniá

connects the harbour here to the dramatic remains of a Venetian castle that protected the town in ancient times. Asos has a small beach; other beautiful beaches lie just around the headland.
◈ *Map H4 • N of Mýrtou Bay, Kefalloniá*

Vathý, Ithaki

The capital and port of Ithaki, Vathý is believed to have been built on the ancient Homeric harbour of Phorkys. Records suggest it was an important trading port in medieval times. In the 17th century, the town's architecture was strongly influenced by the Heptanesian art movement of the day. Although severely damaged in the 1953 earthquake, Vathý was rebuilt, and its whitewashed houses give a sense of its former glory. Some original houses can still be seen. ◈ *Map J4*

Boats moored off Piso Aetós, Ithaki

Piso Aetós, Ithaki

The sleepy port of Piso Aetós lies on an isthmus of land that links north and south Ithaki, and is the arrival point for boats from Kefalloniá. In ancient times, this would have been a livelier place – it was here that the ancient acropolis of Alalkomenes was located. Some believe this port was the site of Odysseus's palace. The beach here is pebbly but pretty.
◈ *Map J4 • W of Vathý, Ithaki*

A Day Trip from Argostóli to Fiskárdo

Morning

🕐 A great day out from Kefallonia's capital, **Argostóli**, is to take the coast road to Fiskárdo village, located at the island's northern tip. After a hearty breakfast at one of Argostóli's tavernas, head north until you begin to see signs for Mýrtou Bay around Agonas. The view of the coastline at this point is breathtaking. Head down the steeply descending road that winds down to the stunning **Mýrtou Bay** and stop for a break. There is a small taverna here, although little else. Refresh yourself, take some photographs and enjoy what is considered to be one of the most beautiful beaches in the world. For great views of the bay from above, go to one of the special viewing areas along the road.

Afternoon

After taking pictures of the bay, head back up the road and follow the signposts towards the village of **Asos**. Lying in an attractive harbour, this village is an ideal place to stop for lunch. There are a handful of good tavernas here that look out over the water. After refreshments, carry on to Fiskárdo. The road goes a little inland through some small and very picturesque hamlets. This part of the journey should only take about 30 minutes; more if you stop to admire the scenery. **Fiskárdo** is a great place to stop and explore before making your way back to Argostóli by retracing your route, or taking the east coast road via **Sámi**.

Left **The small harbour at Póros, Kefalloniá** Right **The harbour village of Frikes, Ithaki**

Best of the Rest

1 Lourdáta, Kefalloniá
Lying on the island's south coast, the picturesque fishing harbour and village of Lourdáta boasts a glorious sand and pebble beach. Nearby is a 13th-century monastery. ◎ *Map H6*
• *Ormos Lourdáta, Kefalloniá*

2 Lake Avythos, Kefalloniá
Surrounded by trees and with Mount Eros in the distance, the large inland lake of Avythos is an enchanting sight. ◎ *Map J5*
• *Near Agios Nikólaos, Kefalloniá*

3 Póros, Kefalloniá
A quiet fishing harbour with a long stretch of beach, a small marina and a few good tavernas, Póros lies in a particularly fertile region. Located near the village is the Monastery of Sissia, the oldest on the island. ◎ *Map J6*
• *Southeast coast, Kefalloniá*

4 Lixoúri, Kefalloniá
An elegant town that flourished in Venetian times, Lixoúri is the island's second-largest community. It sits on the coast overlooking Kefalloniá's capital Argostóli. ◎ *Map G5* • *Pallikí peninsula, Kefalloniá*

5 Kontogenada, Kefalloniá
This small village lies in the centre of the Pallikí peninsula, and is famous as the site of some Mycenaean tombs. It also has a couple of churches with some notable post-Byzantine icons.
◎ *Map G5 • Pallikí peninsula, Kefalloniá*

6 Dia Island, Kefalloniá
Sometimes known as Theionisi, Dia island is the source of many legends. The most popular of these is that it was home to a temple dedicated to the Greek god Zeus. ◎ *Map H6*
• *Off Argostóli, Kefalloniá*

7 Lazareto Island, Ithaki
Once used as a *lazaretto*, or quarantine station, this island, also known as the Island of the Saviour, has a collection of Venetian buildings and a chapel. It is a memorable sight as you pass by on a boat into the harbour at Vathý. ◎ *Map J4 • Off Vathý, Ithaki*

8 Bay of Polis, Ithaki
This is the site of the Loizos cave, where Athena, Artemis and Hera, the Greek goddesses, were believed to have been worshipped in ancient times *(see p37)*.
◎ *Map H4 • Off Stavrós, Ithaki*

9 Frikes, Ithaki
This tiny village is ideal for visitors who want to experience local life. It has a pretty harbour from where ferries regularly ply to Lefkáda and Kefalloniá. ◎ *Map H4*
• *N of Vathý, Ithaki*

10 Perachóri, Ithaki
A monastery dedicated to the Taxiarchs – the Archangels Michael and Gabriel – dominates this small village. Perachóri is also known for its excellent locally produced organic food.
◎ *Map J4 • Near Vathý, Ithaki*

Left **Makrýs Yalos beach, Kefalloniá** Right **Antisamos beach, Kefalloniá**

Beaches

1 Makrýs Yalos Beach, Kefalloniá
The beach of Makrýs Yalos, sometimes spelt Makrýs Gialós, has lovely fine sand and clear and safe water in which to swim. It lies a little way south of Argostóli. ® *Map G6 • Lássi, Kefalloniá*

2 Platýs Yalos Beach, Kefalloniá
Further along the coast from Makrýs Yalos is Platýs Yalos beach, linked to a small island by an isthmus. It has fine sand and is popular with water-sport enthusiasts. ® *Map G6 • Lássi, Kefalloniá*

3 Lepeda Beach, Kefalloniá
Unusual rock formations are a striking sight off Lepeda, a quiet, red-sand beach along the coast south of Lixoúri. The views across the bay to Argostóli are breathtaking. ® *Map G5 • Pallikí peninsula, Kefalloniá*

4 Xi Beach, Kefalloniá
One of the most popular of the Pallikí peninsula's south-coast beaches, Xi has deep red sands and safe swimming waters. It is a short distance from Lixoúri. ® *Map G6 • Pallikí peninsula, Kefalloniá*

5 Antisamos Beach, Kefalloniá
This outstanding beach is one of Sámi's best swimming spots. It is famous for its appearance in the 2001 film, *Captain Corelli's Mandolin (see p17)*. ® *Map J5 • Sámi, Kefalloniá*

6 Agia Effimia Beach, Kefalloniá
The fishing village of Agia Effimia is popular with sailors who moor in its harbour. The beach here, which runs along the east coast, is pebbly but long. ® *Map H5 • Sámi, Kefalloniá*

7 Emplysi Beach, Kefalloniá
One of Fiskárdo's premier beaches, Emplysi emerges at the end of a small track surrounded by olive groves and cypress trees. It lies in a sheltered bay a little over 1 km (half-a-mile) from the village. ® *Map H3 • Fiskárdo, Kefalloniá*

8 Foki Beach, Kefalloniá
Less a beach and more a rocky outcrop, Foki, with its trees that give plenty of shade and clear-blue water, remains one of the most popular spots in the area around Fiskárdo. ® *Map H3 • Fiskárdo, Kefalloniá*

9 Sarakiniko Beach, Ithaki
Popular with swimmers because of its safe waters, this beach lies just west of Vathý. Here you can sit, relax and watch as yachtsmen manoeuvre their boats in and out of the lively anchorage. ® *Map J4 • Vathý, Ithaki*

10 Gidaki Beach, Ithaki
Offering the chance to relax away from the crowds, this beach is accessed only by a hiking track. However, boats do arrive from Vathý every day in summer. ® *Map J4 • Near Vathý, Ithaki*

Left **The church in Travliata, Kefalloniá** Right **Asprogeraka overlooking Póros, Kefalloniá**

🔟 Picturesque Villages

1 Kástro, Kefalloniá
A delightful village, Kástro is characterized by whitewashed Venetian houses and dominated by Agios Georgios, a Byzantine fortress. This unassuming place was once the capital of the island. ✆ *Map H5 • Near Sámi, Kefalloniá*

2 Travliata, Kefalloniá
Life in Travliata, a village in the centre of southern Kefalloniá, revolves around local farming. Views over the surrounding countryside are fabulous. Most of the buildings here were rebuilt after the earthquake of 1953.
✆ *Map H6 • NW of Lourdáta, Kefalloniá*

3 Karyá, Kefalloniá
Karyá is one of several mountain villages, including Vary, Patrikáta and Konitáta, where life appears to have remained unchanged for centuries. The views from this high vantage point are breathtaking. ✆ *Map H4*

4 Lakithra, Kefalloniá
Despite its location near the airport, close to Argostóli town, Lakithra manages to retain its traditional feel. Take in the coastal panoramas at almost every turn.
✆ *Map H6 • Near Argostóli, Kefalloniá*

5 Asprogeraka, Kefalloniá
A quiet village of stone houses surrounded by olive groves, Asprogeraka is famous for being the site of some important Mycenaean wall ruins.
✆ *Map J6 • Inland from Póros, Kefalloniá*

6 Kioni, Ithaki
One of the few villages that was untouched by the 1953 earthquake, Kioni has some lovely centuries-old buildings, including windmills, and has an upmarket feel. ✆ *Map J4 • Near Frikes, Ithaki*

7 Anogi, Ithaki
The attractive Church of the Dormition of the Virgin, adorned with Byzantine frescoes, and its stone houses are what make Anogi special. It is located on Mount Niritos and offers great sea views. ✆ *Map J4 • Near Kioni, Ithaki*

8 Agios Ioannis, Ithaki
The village of Agios Ioannis is one of the most atmospheric and picturesque on the island. Its charming bougainvillea-draped stone houses, tiny streets and fabulous sea views captivate visitors. ✆ *Map H4*

9 Stavrós, Ithaki
The village of Stavrós is Ithaki's second-largest community. Its numerous Venetian houses managed to survive the 1953 earthquake and lend the village its huge charm. ✆ *Map H4 • Bay of Polis, Ithaki*

10 Exogi, Ithaki
Ithaki's northernmost village, Exogi is a remote place. The only thing that can be heard here are the birds. Set high above the coast, it has sensational views out over the water towards Kefalloniá. ✆ *Map H4 • Near Stavrós, Ithaki*

Left **Windsurfing** Right **Cross-country cycling**

Outdoor Activities

1 Nature Trails
Other than the Mount Eros National Park in southern Kefalloniá, the two islands have only a handful of designated nature trails. However, excellent maps are available on both islands to help you chart your own trail.

2 Sailing
Large yachts and motor cruisers can be hired here, provided you possess the right qualifications. Smaller boats, however, are also available at most of the holiday hotspots and are ideal for exploring the little coves dotted around the islands.

3 Swimming
Both islands are blessed with beautifully clear water, and swimming is a popular activity. However, there are strong currents along the west coast, at places such as Mýrtou Bay, where caution should be exercised.

4 Diving and Snorkelling
The indented coastlines of Kefalloniá and Ithaki, with their caves and rocks, are a dream for snorkellers and divers. The clear water in the region means that there is excellent visibility.

5 Archaeological Tours
Hotels often have details of organized archaeological tours to nearby sites. Other places, such as the mosaics at Skála's Roman Villa or the Palaiochóra ruins *(see p37)*, can be explored privately.

6 Cycling
Mountain bikes can be hired on both Kefalloniá and Ithaki, although the nature of the terrain can make cycling a challenging pursuit. However, ordinary bicycles are also available at most hotels and resorts, and from private companies.

7 Golf
There are no 18-hole golf courses on the islands, although this is something that may change in the not-too-distant future. Mini golf, while not as challenging, is a popular activity.

8 Horse Riding
Taking an organized ride into the lush countryside can be a wonderful way to see both islands. There are a few stables and small riding schools that offer this outdoor activity.

9 Water Sports
Beaches such as Makrýs Yalos at Lássi and Lepeda and Xi at Lixoúri *(see p83)*, offer some great water-sports opportunities. Windsurfing and water-skiing are two of the most popular of these activities.

10 Walking
Both Kefalloniá and Ithaki are ideal for people who love walking. Ithaki, especially, has designated hiking paths that take in the island's villages and best views. Details are available from Ithaki's tourist office *(see p102)*.

Left **Patisserie Mavroidis, Kefalloniá** Right **Shop window at Alexander Jewellery, Kefalloniá**

Places to Shop

1 Patisserie Mavroidis, Kefalloniá

Honey-enriched pastries, such as the delicacy baklava, made with layers of filo pastry and nuts, are on sale at this attractive shop. ⊗ *Map G5 • Argostóli, Kefalloniá • 26710 22021 • Open 8am–10pm daily*

2 Chrysa Stamatelatou Book Shop, Kefalloniá

Numerous titles, including fiction and reference books, fill the shelves in this intriguing shop. ⊗ *Map G5 • Argostóli, Kefalloniá • 26710 25070 • Open 9am–2pm, 5pm–late daily*

3 Antonis Cake Shop, Kefalloniá

The confectionery, bread, cakes and pastries on offer here, most made using traditional recipes, are hard to resist. Be sure to try the olive bread. ⊗ *Map H6 • Lakithra, Kefalloniá • 26710 42342 • Open 8am–2:30pm, 5–11pm daily*

4 Olive Press Gift Shop, Kefalloniá

With many branches in Kefalloniá, this popular store sells unusual pieces of jewellery and gifts. ⊗ *Lithóstroto, Argostóli and Lássi, Kefalloniá • 26710 26662 • Open 9am–2pm, 5pm–late daily*

5 Serano, Kefalloniá

Serano serves pastries, ice cream and traditional sweets, such as *glyká*, a candied dessert made from pineapple, melon or walnut. ⊗ *Map G5 • Lixoúri, Kefalloniá • 26710 91257 • Open 9am–late daily*

6 Kefalloniá Images, Kefalloniá

This small shop stocks an assortment of camera equipment, which is useful if you have forgotten your camera or need new batteries. ⊗ *Map J6 • Skála, Kefalloniá • 26710 83295 • Open 9am–2pm, 5pm–late daily*

7 Natasa, Kefalloniá

If you are looking for a unique souvenir, you might just find it here. A range of gifts and wooden furniture is on display. ⊗ *Map H6 • Lakithra, Kefalloniá • 26710 42394 • Open 9am–2pm, 5pm–late daily*

8 Rada Art, Kefalloniá

Rada stocks brightly coloured bowls, figurines and vases along with toys, beads, jewellery, mounted pictures and other gifts. ⊗ *Map G5 • Argostóli, Kefalloniá • 26710 27585 • Open 9am–late daily*

9 Alexander Jewellery, Kefalloniá

Gold and silver necklaces and bracelets, designed in traditional Greek styles, are sold here, along with beads, vases and other gifts. ⊗ *Map H5 • Sámi, Kefalloniá • 26740 22443 • Open 9am–2pm, 5pm–late daily*

10 Spyros Kappatos, Kefalloniá

From contemporary clocks and glass vases to art materials and postcards, the range at this store is extensive. ⊗ *Map G5 • Argostóli, Kefalloniá • 26710 28627 • Open 7am–4pm daily*

Left **Veto Bar, Kefalloniá** Right **Emelisse Art Lounge Bar, Kefalloniá**

Top 10 Cafés and Bars

1 Tavern Nefeli, Kefalloniá
Located in Lássi, Nefeli is a family-run taverna that serves traditional Mediterranean breakfasts, snacks and light meals cooked in its wooden oven. ⊗ *Map G6 • Lássi, Kefalloniá • 26710 25203 • Open 11am–11pm daily*

2 Pikiona Cocktail Bar, Kefalloniá
A contemporary bar set around its own swimming pool and gardens, Pikiona serves breakfast, snacks and beverages during the day, and meals and cocktails in the evening. ⊗ *Map J6 • Skála, Kefalloniá • 26710 83410*

3 Café Bar Muses, Kefalloniá
Big screens showing the day's sports events, good music and a menu of cocktails, coffees and snacks ensure this bar is always lively. ⊗ *Map H6 • Lourdáta, Kefalloniá • 26710 31175 • Open 8am–late daily*

4 Veto Bar, Kefalloniá
The large, bright Veto bar is known for its cocktails. It offers light snacks and beers as well as sports events on television screens. ⊗ *Map J6 • Skála, Kefalloniá • 26710 83015 • Open 11am–late daily*

5 San Giorgio Bar, Kefalloniá
This lively pool bar is open most hours of the day. It serves a range of drinks, cocktails and light snacks, such as *souvláki* and salads. ⊗ *Map J6 • Skála, Kefalloniá • 26710 83267 • Open 9am–12:30am daily*

6 Emelisse Art Lounge Bar, Kefalloniá
This stylish bar overlooks Emblissi bay and serves drinks, cocktails and light snacks based on local recipes. ⊗ *Map H4 • Emblissi bay, Fiskárdo, Kefalloniá • 26740 41200 • Open 8am–late daily*

7 Erissos Palace Bar, Kefalloniá
Located within Fiskárdo's Erissos Palace Hotel, this bar is open to non-residents. It serves an assortment of drinks and snacks based on traditional Kefallonián recipes, best enjoyed by the pool. ⊗ *Map H4 • Maganos, Fiskárdo, Kefalloniá • 26740 41350 • Open 8am–late daily*

8 Volto Bar, Kefalloniá
Plush interiors gives this bar in the Hotel Méditerranée *(see p114)* an atmospheric feel. Coffee blends, light snacks, ice creams and cocktails are all served.

9 Porto Skála Bar and Beach Bar, Kefalloniá
These two bars serve the usual range of drinks and light snacks, best enjoyed on the terrace. ⊗ *Map J6 • Porto Skála Hotel, Skála, Kefalloniá • 26710 83501 • Open 11am–late daily*

10 Para thin'alos, Ithaki
This café takes inspiration from the French, both in terms of its decor and menu. Light dishes and French wine are served all day long. ⊗ *Map J4 • Vathý, Ithaki • 26740 33567 • Open 11am–5pm daily*

Left **Premier Restaurant, Kefalloniá** Right **The Pines Restaurant, Kefalloniá**

TOP 10 Restaurants

1 Tassia
Run by Tassia Dendrinou, a cook-book author, this eatery is famed for its fine seafood dishes and wine list. ⊗ *Map H4 • Fiskárdo Harbour, Kefalloniá • 26740 41205 • Open 11am–late daily • €€€€*

2 Chinese House
With an extensive menu inspired by the Orient and decor to match, the Chinese House offers an alternative to traditional taverna fare. ⊗ *Map G6 • Lássi, Kefalloniá • 26710 24815 • Open 6pm–late daily • €€€*

3 The Olive Tree
This attractive restaurant overlooks the countryside. It specializes in *nouvelle cuisine grecque* – beautifully presented Greek food and offers fine wine and great cocktails. ⊗ *Map H6 • Lakithra, Kefalloniá • 26710 31577 • Open 6pm–late daily • €€€€*

4 Aquarius Restaurant
The Aquarius serves dishes such as veal *stifado*, and *chicken a la Romana* (chicken stuffed with tomatoes and feta cheese). ⊗ *Map J6 • Skála, Kefalloniá • 26710 83612 • Open 6pm–late daily • €€€€*

5 Pikiona Restaurant
A bright, lively place serving light meals and classic dishes all day long, beachside Pikiona stands in its own gardens, beside a swimming pool. ⊗ *Map J6 • Skála, Kefalloniá • 26710 83410 • Open 8am–late daily • €€€*

6 Oskars Complex
Barbecued fish and meat along with an à la carte menu are offered at this seafront restaurant. It is well known for its Greek party nights. ⊗ *Map G6 • Lássi, Kefalloniá • 26710 23438 • Open noon–late daily • €€€*

7 Premier Restaurant
The Premier has stylish decor, a menu of Greek classics and some tempting cakes and desserts. ⊗ *Map G5 • Plateia Valianou, Argostóli, Kefalloniá • 26710 23280 • Open 7am–2pm daily • €€€*

8 Sea Pearl Restaurant
This elegant restaurant has both indoor and alfresco-style dining. Meals are served all day long. ⊗ *Map J6 • Apostolata Elios Resort, Skála, Kefalloniá • 26710 83581 • Open 7am–late daily • €€€€*

9 Cefalonia Garden Restaurant
Breakfast, lunch and evening meals are offered to both guests and non-residents at this chic contemporary resort restaurant. ⊗ *Map G5 • Cefalonia Garden Village, Agios Giannis, Kefalloniá • 26710 94405 • Open 6:30am–late daily • €€€*

10 The Pines Restaurant
This bougainvillea-covered place, with a terrace boasting lovely views, is a popular brunch and dinner venue. The cuisine is a mix of international and local. ⊗ *Map J6 • Skála, Kefalloniá • 26710 83216 • Open 9am–late daily • €€€€*

Price Categories

For a three-course meal for one with half a bottle of wine (or equivalent meal), taxes and extra charges.

€	under €20
€€	€20–€30
€€€	€30–€40
€€€€	€40–€50
€€€€€	over €50

Patsouras, Kefalloniá

Traditional Tavernas

Patsouras
The local dish *krasáto* – pork cooked in wine and herbs – is a speciality of this taverna. Be sure to dine on the pretty terrace here. ◈ *Map G5 • Metaxas St, Argostóli, Kefalloniá • 26710 20061 • Open noon–late daily • €€*

Platanos
A huge *platanos* (plane) tree provides shade to diners enjoying fresh dishes cooked to perfection at this seafood restaurant. There are grills and salads on the menu too. ◈ *Map H4 • Asos, Kefalloniá • 26740 51381 • Open 11am–late daily • €€*

Kantouni
Kantouni offers a wide range of beautifully presented grills and seafood. Try one of its casseroles, based on local recipes. ◈ *Map J4 • Limani, Vathý, Ithaki • 26740 32918 • Open noon–late daily • €€€*

Alexis
With its brightly coloured exterior, Alexis is a landmark restaurant. Its menu includes classic local dishes, excellent seafood and fine wines. ◈ *Map H4 • Main Square, Fiskárdo, Kefalloniá • 26740 41212 • Open 11am–late daily • €€€€€*

Grivas Taverna
A popular taverna for well over 75 years, the Grivas offers a taste of rural Kefalloniá in the heart of town. Its menu is traditional Greek. ◈ *Map G5 • Vasil Vandoru 1, Argostóli, Kefalloniá • 26710 24259 • Open 11am–5:30pm • €€*

Hersona's Taverna
The owner of this popular taverna is the village butcher, which explains why top-class local meat is the main ingredient on its menu. ◈ *Map H6 • Troianata, Kefalloniá • 26710 69940 • Open 6pm–late daily • €€€*

Taverna Drosia
A mix of traditional Greek and Venezuelan dishes is served at this taverna. Its hill-side setting affords good views of the harbour. ◈ *Map J4 • Vathý, Ithaki • 26740 32959 • Open 6pm–late daily • €€€€*

Paliocaravo
Run by the local Vlisma family, this is one of the oldest restaurants in Vathý. Classic Greek dishes and fresh fish are served accompanied by fine wines. ◈ *Map J4 • Limani, Vathý, Ithaki • 26740 32573 • Open 7:30am–late daily • €€€€*

Cephalonia Palace Beach Taverna
Overlooking Xi beach and the ocean, this taverna is known for its excellent menu of snacks, local dishes and à la carte favourites. ◈ *Map G6 • Cephanlonia Palace Beach, Xi beach, Kefalloniá • 26710 93190 • Open 10am–6pm • €€€€*

Taverna Rompolis
This taverna is known for its superb wine and a menu based on recipes handed down through the generations. ◈ *Map H5 • Poulata, Sámi, Kefalloniá • 26740 23323 • Open 6pm–late daily • €€€*

Left **Charming Maherádo** Right **The hilltop village of Keri**

Zákynthos

ZÁKYNTHOS IS THE SOUTHERNMOST *of the Ionian islands, and is characterized by high mountains clothed in cypress trees and fabulous sandy beaches, including the iconic Navagio and Laganás, home to the endangered loggerhead turtle (Caretta caretta). The island boasts an extraordinary number of sea caves, the most famous being the beautiful Blue Grotto. Zákynthos is believed to have been inhabited since ancient times, although few original structures still stand. Its capital, Zákynthos Town, and most of its smaller towns and villages were all but destroyed in the 1953 earth-quake that shook Greece and its islands, and have been rebuilt in recent times.*

Gulf of Laganás

🔟 Sights

1. Zákynthos Town
2. Byzantine Museum
3. Blue Caves
4. Keri
5. Gulf of Laganás
6. Volímes
7. Navagio Beach
8. Anafonítria
9. Melinado
10. Maherádo

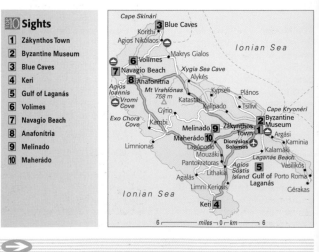

Venetian-style buildings, Zákynthos Town

Zákynthos Town
One of many elegant squares that characterize Zákynthos Town is its hub, Plateia Solomóu, from where most sights can be reached easily. Highlights include the Museum of Solomós, the Naval Museum of Zákynthos, which explores Greece's maritime history, and the fabulous Church of St Dionýsios, dedicated to the island's patron saint. After suffering earthquake damage, the town has been rebuilt in a Neo-Classical style reminiscent of its Venetian period *(see pp20–21)*.

Byzantine Museum
A scale model of a pre-earthquake Zákynthos Town is on display at this superb museum, along with icons and frescoes saved from some of the churches and monasteries damaged during the earthquake. Important exhibits include *Descent from the Cross*, a painting from the Church of St Andreas of the Gardens; the imposing 17th-century gilded templon from the Church of St Demetrios of Kola; and a collection of sculptures dating from Hellenic and Byzantine times *(see pp22–3)*.

Blue Caves
The Blue Caves, formed by the incessant action of the sea on the coastline, lie at the northern tip of Zákynthos. The main cave, Blue Grotto, is overlooked by a picturesque lighthouse, and is an extraordinary complex comprising two caverns that were discovered in the late 1900s. The caves look particularly breathtaking when the sun's rays shine in, turning the shimmering water a vivid shade of sapphire. They can be reached on a boat from the village of Agios Nikólaos. ◈ *Map K1 • Cape Skinári, Zákynthos*

Keri
The picturesque village of Keri, with its original stone houses built along meandering narrow alleyways, lies high up in the hills to the south of the island. Keri is one of the few villages that escaped the 1953 earthquake, and is popular with visitors keen to experience the centuries-old lifestyle of the people of Zákynthos. Surrounded by vineyards and olive groves, the village produces some of the best wine and olive oil on the island. It offers great views of the sea and the coastline. ◈ *Map L3 • Limni Kerious beach, Zákynthos*

The breathtaking Blue Grotto

A tunnel full of marine life is a highlight of diving at the Keri caves near Keri village.

Around Zakynthos

Dionýsios Solomós

The patron saint of Zákynthos, St Dionýsios, was a monk at the Monastery of Virgin Anafonítria *(see p40–41)* in the 16th century. He later became an Orthodox Christian Archbishop in Aegina, following a trip to the Holy Land. His remains are housed in a silver coffin in the Church of St Dionýsios in Zákynthos Town.

Pretty Anafonítria

Gulf of Laganás

While it often throngs with water-sports enthusiasts, the Gulf of Laganás is better known as the breeding ground of the endangered loggerhead turtle *(Caretta caretta)*. The turtles mate at sea and the females come ashore to lay their eggs at Laganás beach *(see p94)*. The Sea Turtle Protection Association helps protect the breeding ground.
◈ *Map M3 • Off Laganás, Zákynthos*

Volímes

An attractive village with its original architecture intact, Volímes lies in the island's mountainous northwest region, a little inland from Navagio beach. It is divided in two – Ano (upper) and Kato (lower) Volímes. Its enchanting Venetian Baroque St Paraskevi church has a gilded iconostasis and good examples of ecclesiastical art. Volímes' textile craftsmanship is famous.
◈ *Map K1 • Northwest Zákynthos*

Navagio Beach

Lying in a sheltered cove with soaring cliffs on either side, Navagio beach is world-famous. A trip to Zákynthos would not be complete without visiting this fine white-sand beach. Also known as Shipwreck Bay, which refers to the freighter that sits partially buried in the sand, the beach is reached by road from Volímes, or by boat. ◈ *Map K1 • West coast, Zákynthos*

Anafonítria

With its vineyards and vine-covered houses, this pretty mountain village is best known for its connections to Dionýsios Solomós, the island's patron saint *(see p31)*, who was a monk at the Monastery of the Virgin Anafonítria *(see pp40–41)*. This well-preserved building has a medieval tower and a small church. Although dimly lit, one can make out the church's ornate carved wooden iconostasis.
◈ *Map K2 • Near Volímes, Zákynthos*

The scenic village of Volímes

9 Melinado

A traditional community in the heart of the island, the village of Melinado is surrounded by olive groves. Occupying an elevated position, it has outstanding views of the surrounding countryside and the plains below. A mighty temple dedicated to the Greek goddess Artemis once stood in the village, the remains of which can be seen today. Recent excavations have unearthed many major finds, including architectural detailing and ancient coins. The ruins of a church lie here as well. ⌖ Map L2
• Near Lagópodo, Zákynthos

The church ruins at Melinado

10 Maherádo

The large village of Maherádo has been an agricultural community for centuries. Its centrepiece is a 14th-century church with a Venetian bell tower. Dedicated to St Mavra, a saint revered by the islanders, the Church of Agia Mavra has a notable collection of brightly coloured wall and ceiling frescoes, a lavish iconostasis and many icons. One of the icons, called the Agia Mavra, is thought to be miraculous and worshippers kiss it as a mark of respect.
⌖ Map L2 • Near Melinado, Zákynthos

A Day Trip from Zákynthos Town

Morning

Start your day in the capital, Zákynthos Town, with a good breakfast at one of the many great tavernas on **Plateia Solomoú**. After breakfast, head north towards **Cape Kryonéri** (see p96) along the coast road, which offers breathtaking views of the Ionian Sea. Take in the resort of **Tsiliví** (see p94) en route, where you can stop for a cool drink and snack in one of its tavernas. Next comes the village-cum-resort of **Plános** (see p96), before arriving in **Alykés** (see p94). A superb resort that is popular with wind-surfers, Alykés offers a wide selection of traditional tavernas. Stop here for lunch before continuing your journey.

Afternoon

Leaving Alykés and its lively holiday-makers behind, head inland to the island's largest village, **Katastári** (see p94). After leaving Katastári and driving north a short distance, you will arrive at a junction. You can either head west to **Volímes** or continue north on another, smaller mountainous road. You will see amazing scenery and coastal views if you take the smaller road, passing the famous **Xygia Sea Cave** (see p94), with its sulphurous spring. Next, if you plan to see the **Blue Caves** from the sea, look out for the signposts to **Agios Nikólaos** (see p34), where you can catch a boat. After taking in the excellent views of the Blue Caves, head back via Volímes or retrace your steps along the coast.

Left **Magnificent Mount Vrahiónas** Right **Holiday-makers on the beach at Alykés**

🔟 Best of the Rest

1 Xygia Sea Cave
The Xygia Sea Cave and beach is famed for its natural sulphurous springs. It is said that swimming in these waters is therapeutic. ◈ *Map L1 • Off Xygia beach, Zákynthos*

2 Strofades Islands
The Strofades islands – Arpia, Stamfani and a few small islets – lie about 60 km (37 miles) south of Zákynthos. They are part of the Zákynthos National Sea Park. ◈ *Map M2 • SE of Zákynthos*

3 Laganás Beach
This beach is the site where the loggerhead turtle comes ashore to lay eggs from June to August. The eggs are laid in deep holes and covered with sand. ◈ *Map M3 • Gulf of Laganás, Zákynthos*

4 Katastári
Katastári is the largest village on the island. The buildings on its main street were built to follow the contours of the terrain down to the sea, giving the village the appearance of an amphitheatre. It offers stunning views of Alykés bay. ◈ *Map L2 • Near Alykés, Zákynthos*

5 Alykés
The resort of Alykés is an ideal destination for families. Its numerous tavernas, long stretches of sandy beach, shallow water and varied water sports keep both adults and children entertained. ◈ *Map L2 • Near Xygia beach, east coast, Zákynthos*

6 Tsiliví
Along with Alykés, the east-coast resort of Tsiliví is a magnet for holiday-makers. It boasts tavernas, restaurants, beaches, family attractions and a good selection of hotels. ◈ *Map L2 • Near Zákynthos Town, Zákynthos*

7 Kambi
If you want to experience a true Zákynthos sunset, then this traditional village is the place to go. Head up the hill till you reach a big cross and wait for the sun to set – it is a spectacular sight. ◈ *Map K2 • West coast, Zákynthos*

8 Mount Vrahiónas
The 758-m- (2,500-ft-) tall Mount Vrahiónas is the highest point on Zákynthos. It lies at the centre of the island and is clothed in trees. Tiny villages, such as Gýrio and Loúha, are located around it. ◈ *Map K2*

9 Kalipado
With its traditional stone houses, pretty churches and narrow streets, the village of Kalipado has changed little over the years. ◈ *Map L2 • NW of Zákynthos Town, Zákynthos*

10 Agios Ioannis Island
Lying off the west coast at the entrance to Vromi cove, this isolated off-the-beaten-track island is a haven for wildlife. From here you can enjoy great veiws of the coastline of Zákynthos. ◈ *Map K2 • W of Zákynthos*

Left **A roadside taverna at Ambelokipoi** Right **Agios Sóstis island and its bridge**

🔟 Picturesque Villages

1 Lagópodo
A small village surrounded by olive groves, Lagópodo is the place to head to if you want some peace and quiet. It is located near the village of Maherádo. ✆ *Map L2 • Mount Vrahiónas foothills, Zákynthos*

2 Ambelokipoi
Largely a farming community, Ambelokipoi is delightful and has great mountain views. It is conveniently located near the island's airport and Zákynthos Town. ✆ *Map L2 • SE of Zákynthos Town*

3 Lithakia
The charming hamlet of Lithakia is a resort in the making. The beach is quiet, the sea is shallow, and the handful of tavernas here are gradually growing in number. ✆ *Map L3 • Gulf of Laganás, Zákynthos*

4 Agalás
The rugged coastline and forested valleys that characterize the southwest of Zákynthos form a scenic backdrop to this village. A traditional community, Agalás is known for preserving age-old customs. ✆ *Map L3 • N of Keri, Zákynthos*

5 Pantokratoras
Quiet and scenic, this village, set in a verdant landscape of olive trees, provides visitors with the best of both worlds – a traditional way of life and a beach just a short distance away. ✆ *Map L3 • Near Lithakia, Zákynthos*

6 Mouzáki
Established in the early 1500s, the unspoilt village of Mouzáki has a long history. Many traditions have been kept alive in this small community. ✆ *Map L3 • N of Pantokratoras, Zákynthos*

7 Romiri
A remote village blessed with panoramic views of the countryside to the east and the mountains to the west, Romiri is traditional and quiet. ✆ *Map L2 • N of Mouzáki, Zákynthos*

8 Kalamáki
Lying on the south coast, Kalamáki boasts one of the best beaches along this stretch of coastline. The village has fine sand and the sea here is shallow, making Kalamáki a favourite destination for families. ✆ *Map M3 • Gulf of Laganás, Zákynthos*

9 Laganás
Best-known for its nightclubs, bars and lively visitors, this village is, in fact, a traditional community. Fishing was the only industry in Laganás before the advent of tourism. ✆ *Map L3 • Gulf of Laganás, Zákynthos*

10 Agios Sóstis Island
Linked to the shores of Laganás by a bridge, Agios Sóstis is a small island. It is popular with families due to its beautiful beach and calm waters, which are ideal for swimming. ✆ *Map L3 • Gulf of Laganás, S of Zákynthos*

Left **Vromi cove** Right **Porto Zoro beach**

🔟 Beaches, Coves and Resorts

1 Vromi Cove
A delightful indentation on the west coast, Vromi cove can be reached only by a small road from the village of Anafonítria. Aghios Ioannis island *(see p94)* lies at its entrance. Ⓢ *Map K2*
• *West coast, Zákynthos*

2 Exo Chora Cove
The cove at the west-coast town of Exo Chora is quiet and unassuming. The town itself is a pleasure to visit, and has many original houses that survived the 1953 earthquake. Ⓢ *Map K2*
• *Exo Chora, Zákynthos*

3 Cape Kryonéri
Lying on the east coast about 1-km- (half-a-mile) north of Zákynthos Town, Cape Kryonéri has a narrow pebble beach that runs down to the sea. Ⓢ *Map M2*
• *Near Zákynthos Town, Zákynthos*

4 Plános
Although a small village, Plános is fast developing into a popular holiday destination. It is one of the the liveliest resorts on the east coast, with a soft sandy beach and calm water. Ⓢ *Map L2*
• *Near Zákynthos Town, Zákynthos*

5 Argási
Located on the east coast, south of Zákynthos Town, Argási is a lively resort that has managed to retain its historic charm. It has a good selection of excellent tavernas. Ⓢ *Map M2*
• *S of Zákynthos Town, Zákynthos*

6 Kaminia Beach
Located on the island's southernmost tip is the quiet and undeveloped Kamínia beach, which offers good views of the tree-covered headland.
Ⓢ *Map M2* • *Near Argási, Zákynthos*

7 Porto Zoro Beach
If you love snorkelling, then the striking rock formations at this quiet east-coast beach are worth exploring. It is considered to be one of the best beaches on the Vasilikós peninsula. Ⓢ *Map M3*
• *Vasilikós peninsula, Zákynthos*

8 Vasilikós
The small village of Vasilikós is renowned for its great beaches, rugged coastline and excellent swimming conditions. It is the main community on the Vasilikós peninsula, to the island's south.
Ⓢ *Map M3* • *Vasilikós peninsula, Zákynthos*

9 Porto Roma
A tiny fishing harbour with a small pebbly beach and a handful of tavernas, Porto Roma lies on the southeast coast of the island. It is well known for its peaceful ambience. Ⓢ *Map M3*
• *Vasilikós peninsula, Zákynthos*

10 Gérakas Beach
Often referred to as the largest beach on the island, Gérakas, with its long sweep of golden sands, is also one of the best. The beach lies on the southernmost tip of Zákynthos.
Ⓢ *Map M3* • *Cape Gérakas, Zákynthos*

Left **Swimming** Right **Jet-skiing**

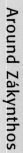

Outdoor Activities

1 Nature Trails
Following a nature trail or creating your own can be a wonderful way to explore Zákynthos. Be sure to take a good, detailed map, walking shoes and plenty of water.

2 Sailing
With minimal tidal variation and the gentle Mediterranean *maïstro* wind blowing, the sea around Zákynthos is ideal for sailing enthusiasts. There are numerous places to anchor on the island, and a marina at the port in Zákynthos Town (see pp26–7).

3 Swimming
Swimming is a popular activity at the island's beaches, and is generally safe. However, it is important to be aware that some beaches may shelve dramatically. Those on the east and south coast are generally safer.

4 Diving and Snorkelling
The island's rugged coastline presents some fine opportunities for snorkellers to explore. Diving hotspots include the Keri caves (see p91) and Kalamáki (see p95).

5 Archaeological Tours
The island has many historic sites, such as Zákynthos Town's Venetian fortress (see pp20–21) and the ruins of a temple dedicated to Artemis at Melinado (see p93). You can visit these on your own or go on an organized tour, available at most resorts.

6 Cycling
Most resorts have companies offering bicycles and mountain bikes for hire, but be aware that the rugged terrain can make cycling a difficult activity. Be sure to take plenty of water and a mobile phone with you.

7 Golf
Apart from mini-golf centres, such as Alykés Mini Golf (see p44), dotted around the island – some challenging, some less so – there are no major golf courses here. However, full 18-hole courses are being discussed.

8 Horse Riding
Stables and small riding schools, such as Akrotiri Horse Riding Farm (see p47), can be found around the island. Several of these schools lie near Laganás (see p95) and Alykés (see p44).

9 Water Sports
Most major resorts offer all the usual water sports, including windsurfing, water-skiing and jet-skiing. However, there may be restrictions around the breeding grounds of the endangered loggerhead turtle (see p92), so visitors should be cautious in such areas.

10 Walking
Some of the towns and villages have designated walking routes. Alternatively, you can take a detailed map and devise your very own route. A popular hike is from Plános to Alykés (see p47).

Left **Outdoor seating at the Base Café, Zákynthos Town** Right **Sign for the Olympic Bar, Alýkes**

ᴛᴏᴘ10 Cafés and Bars

1 The Cave Bar
Literally set in a cave, with a castle behind it and overlooking Gulf of Laganás, this bar is full of atmosphere. It offers subtle music, good cocktails and nibbles. ◈ *Map M3 • Kalamáki, Zákynthos • 26950 41044 • Open noon–late daily*

2 Miami Bar
A super beach bar, Miami serves burgers with salad, pizzas with fries, and ice cream, plus a wide choice of breakfast options and cocktails throughout the day. ◈ *Map L2 • Tsiliví, Zákynthos • 26950 45982 • Open 7am–5pm daily*

3 Pierros Beach Bar
A landmark beachside bar, Pierros serves hearty breakfasts and snacks throughout the day, plus cocktails when the sun goes down. ◈ *Map L3 • Vezal, Gulf of Laganás, Zákynthos • 69728 23565 • Open 8:30am–late daily*

4 Base Café
More than just a café, Base is an institution in Zákynthos Town. It serves local drinks, such as ouzo, as well as cocktails and light snacks. ◈ *Map L4 • Plateia Agiou Markou, Zákynthos Town, Zákynthos • 26950 42409 • Open 9am–late daily*

5 Banana Beach Bar
Looking out over the Ionian Sea's crystal-clear water, this superb beach bar serves refreshing drinks all day long. ◈ *Map M3 • Banana Beach, Vasilikós Peninsula, Zákynthos • Open 10am–6pm daily*

6 Paradise Cocktail Bar
Served with a large helping of live music and fun, fabulous cocktails are offered at the Paradise, which has been around for over 20 years. ◈ *Map L2 • Tsiliví, Zákynthos • 26950 23190 • Open 6pm–late daily*

7 Paporo
The beach bar at Paporo is open during the day for refreshments, while in the evening you can enjoy cocktails and snacks from its creative menus. ◈ *Map L2 • Paporo Centre, Alykés, Zákynthos • 26950 83950 • Open 11am–late daily*

8 Irish Bar
With a large terrace and olive and palm gardens, the popular Irish Bar serves local beers, spirits and cocktails. ◈ *Map L2 • Alykés Crossroad, Zákynthos • 26950 83727 • Open 6pm–late daily*

9 Planet Pub
You can dance to a variety of music, swim in the well-lit pool or simply enjoy lively conversation over cocktails and light snacks at this landmark bar. ◈ *Map L2 • Tsiliví, Zákynthos • 26950 45106 • Open 6pm–late daily*

10 Olympic Bar
With contemporary, quirky decor, this stylish lounge bar offers local Greek drinks, such as ouzo, *tsipouro* and raki, cocktails and café-style cuisine. ◈ *Map L2 • Alykés, Zákynthos • 26950 83507 • Open 6pm–late daily*

Price Categories

For a three-course
meal for one with half
a bottle of wine (or
equivalent meal), taxes
and extra charges.

€ under €20
€€ €20–€30
€€€ €30–€40
€€€€ €40–€50
€€€€€ over €50

Above **The veranda at Rominos**

Places to Eat

1 Zakanthi Restaurant
Hearty grills and local dishes, such as *souvláki* and salads, are on Zakanthi's menu. You can eat indoors or enjoy dining alfresco-style in the lush, subtly lit garden. ◈ *Map M3 • Kalamáki, Zákynthos • 26950 43586 • Open 9am–late daily • €€*

2 Mouria Restaurant
This elegant restaurant serves seafood platters, such as mussels with fine wine, and other delicacies. ◈ *Map M3 • Laganás beach, Zákynthos • 26950 51113 • Open noon–late daily • €€€€*

3 Flocas Café
One of Argási's most stylish venues, the popular Flocas serves breakfast, including savoury and sweet crepes and pancakes, and other meals throughout the day. ◈ *Map M2 • Argási, Zákynthos • 26950 24848 • Open 11am–late daily • €€€*

4 Buon Amici
Known for its creatively presented dishes, including pasta, seafood and meat in the finest Italian sauces, Buon Amici can be found in Kalamáki's main street. ◈ *Map M3 • Kalamáki, Zákynthos • 26950 22915 • Open 6pm–late daily • €€€€*

5 Dennis Taverna
Located in the centre of Lithakia, Dennis Taverna is easy to find. This family-run taverna serves delicious Greek dishes that have stood the test of time. ◈ *Map L3 • Lithakia, Zákynthos • 26950 51387 • Open 6pm–late daily • €€€*

6 Lofos Restaurant
Built in stone to reflect the island's traditional architecture, the Lofos is a gem in the heart of Zákynthos. The food is authentic Greek. ◈ *Map L2 • Meso Gerakari, Near Katastári, Zákynthos • 26950 62643 • Open 6pm–late daily • €€€€*

7 Dionisos Taverna
Dionisos is known for its menu of international and local home-made dishes, with ingredients fresh from its garden. It offers alfresco dining on its terrace. ◈ *Map L2 • Alikanás, near Alykés, Zákynthos • 26950 83954 • Open 11am–late daily • €€€*

8 La Bella Napoli
Enjoy the flavours of Italy at the La Bella Napoli, with pizza and pasta dishes accompanied by fine Italian wines and soft music. ◈ *Map L3 • Laganás, Zákynthos • 09461 67018 • Open 11am–late daily • €€€€*

9 Spitiko Taverna
Local Greek and Zákynthian cuisine are the specialties at this contemporary eatery. Choose from its mezes or fish platters, *kleftiko* and *souvláki*. ◈ *Map M2 • Zákynthos Town, Zákynthos • 26950 41519 • Open 6pm–late daily • €€€*

10 Rominos
A lively restaurant offering Mexican, Italian and local Greek cuisine, Rominos has something to suit every palate. ◈ *Map L2 • Tsiliví, Zákynthos • 26950 51900 • Open noon–late daily • €€€*

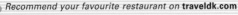

STREETSMART

CORFU & THE IONIANS' TOP 10

Left **Beach umbrellas offering protection from the sun** Right **Two different euro coins**

TOP 10 Planning Your Trip

1 When to Go
The Ionians are primarily a spring and summer destination, with temperatures averaging 26°C in July and August. Winters can be quite mild, with average temperatures of around 10°C. Rain, and occasionally snow, can fall in the winter months, especially in the mountains.

2 Which Island
Each island has its own distinctive style. The bigger islands are ideal for visitors who love the beach, water sports and nightlife, while the smaller islands offer nature walks and quiet relaxation. Inland, all islands have a traditional way of life.

3 Tourist Offices
There are information and tourist police offices that assist with enquiries in all the main towns. However, just walking in to obtain information is not always appreciated. Most expect you to ask for information over the telephone, but enquiry desks at airports are an exception to this.

4 Passports and Visas
Citizens of the EU, USA, Canada, Australia and New Zealand only need a valid passport for a stay of up to 90 days. No visa is required. Citizens from other countries should consult the Greek embassy in their home country before leaving for Greece to make sure that they have the necessary documentation.

5 Customs
While restrictions are imposed on the amount of money that can be imported or exported, duty-paid goods for personal use, such as alcohol and perfume, are not subject to strict limits within the EU. However, the removal of archaeological artifacts is strictly prohibited. Non-EU citizens may be spot-checked.

6 Currency
The local currency is the euro (€). Euro coins come in 1, 2, 5, 10, 20 and 50 cents and €1 and €2. Banknotes come in €5, €10, €20, €50, €100, €200 and €500 denominations. Visitors may bring in any amount of foreign currency, but large sums must be declared.

7 What to Take
Take any prescribed medicines in a volume suitable for the length of stay, along with electrical adaptors, sun screen and aftersun. Pack sportswear, beachwear, smart casuals and a hat, and a jumper for cool evenings.

8 Electricity
The standard current is 230V (50 Hz) and the plugs have two or three round pins. Transformers and adapters required for certain American and British appliances are not easily available in Greece, so be sure to pack these.

9 Children
The islands are very child-friendly and nappies and other products are readily available. Children are particularly at risk of sunburn (see p107) so take extra care.

10 Weddings
Getting married in a civil ceremony here is a simple affair, but church formalities vary between islands. Before the wedding, documents, such as birth certificates, must be produced.

Tourist Offices

Corfu
Corfu Town: 26610 37520 (tourist information); 26610 39503 (tourist police)

Paxí
Gáios: 26620 32222 (tourist information)

Lefkáda
Lefkáda Town: 26450 29370 (tourist police)

Kefalloniá
Argostóli: 26710 22248 (tourist information)

Itháki
Vathý: 26740 32969 (tourist information)

Zákynthos
Zákynthos Town: 26950 25428 (tourist information); 26950 24482 (tourist police)

Preceding pages **Souvenir shop, Gáios, Paxí**

Left **A ferry plying between the islands** Right **Bus service, Kefalloniá**

Top 10 Getting There and Around

1 Package Holidays
Package tours to the islands include outward and inward flights, accommodation and transfers to and from the airports. Specialist walking, sailing, diving and wedding packages are also offered.

2 By Scheduled Flight
Olympic Airlines and Aegean Air serve the Ionians, although most flights are domestic. Scheduled flights arrive at the airports at Corfu, Kefalloniá and Zákynthos from Elefthérios Venizélos International Airport in Athens. Direct low-cost flights are also available.

3 By Charter Flight
Charter flights, run by specialist tour operators, fly to the airports at Corfu, Kefalloniá and Zákynthos from around the world. Some fly all year round, while others have limited service in winter.

4 By Boat
Regular ferries from Italy and the Greek ports of Igoumenitsa, Sayada, Thesprotia and Patras serve Corfu and Paxí. Ferries ply between Ithaki, Lefkáda and Kefalloniá. Kefalloniá is linked to Kyllini, Astakos and Patras on the mainland. Kyllini also serves Zákynthos.

5 By Yacht
There are a number of marinas and anchorages, including Corfu's Limin Kerkira Marina and Gouvia Marina, the well-equipped Lefkáda Marina, Argostóli Marina in Kefalloniá and Port Zákynthos Marina in Zákynthos (see pp26–7).

6 By Cruise Ship
Corfu and the Ionians appear on many cruise-ship itineraries. These floating hotels can often be seen anchored off the coast of Corfu Town or at Port Zákynthos. Cruise ships depart regularly from Lefkáda, Kefalloniá, Ithaki, Paxí and Antipaxí.

7 Car Hire
A full driving licence held for at least a year is mandatory to hire a vehicle. All leading car-hire companies have offices at major resorts and airports. It is possible to hire 4WDs for off-road explorations or minibuses for group trips.

8 Rules of the Road
Highways tend to be in good order, but be careful in mountainous terrain or rural areas. Driving is on the right, and speed limits must be followed. Children under 12 must not travel in the front.

9 By Bus
Short bus trips between the villages offer an old-world charm; most are older-style buses running to a fairly infrequent timetable. Larger towns have an internal bus network and intercity buses to Athens that include the ferry fare.

10 By Taxi
Taxis are easy to find on the islands. The main towns have dedicated taxi ranks and smaller villages have vehicles for hire. Taxis are metered and inexpensive, but negotiate beforehand if you want one for a longer duration.

Airports

Ioannis Kapodistrias Airport, Corfu
Map N3 • 26610 89600

Kefalloniá International Airport
Map H6 • 26710 29900

Dionysios Solomós Airport, Zákynthos
Map M2 • 26950 29500

Ports

Corfu
• Corfu Town: Map N4; 26610 40002

Paxí
• Gáios: Map B5; 26620 32259

Lefkáda
• Lefkáda Town: Map J1; 26450 22322
• Nydrí: Map J2; 26450 92509

Kefalloniá
• Argostóli: Map G5; 26710 22224
• Sámi: Map H5; 26740 22031

Ithaki
• Vathý: Map J4; 26740 32909

Zákynthos
• Zákynthos Town: Map M2; 26950 28117

Sea crossings are more frequent during summer months.

Left **An ATM** Centre **Post box, with its distinctive yellow colour** Right **An OTE pay phone**

Banking and Communications

1 Money
As with mainland Greece, the Ionians adopted the European currency, the euro *(see p102)*, in 2001, replacing the longstanding currency, the drachma. Changing money to euros is simple, even in smaller towns, with banks and *bureaux de change* offering decent exchange rates.

2 Banks
Banking hours are 8am–2pm on weekdays except Fridays, when the hours are 8am–1:30pm. Banks are usually closed in the afternoons and on Saturdays. However, in the major tourist areas, some banks have adopted longer opening hours, especially during summer.

3 ATMs
ATMs operate round the clock and accept most major cards. Although machines are usually only found in the main towns and busy tourist areas, they are increasingly being installed in smaller towns and villages.

4 Credit Cards
Almost all hotels, restaurants and shops accept MasterCard, Visa, Diner's Club and American Express credit cards, and major debit cards. Smaller establishments prefer cash or cheques and village shops or tavernas rarely accept credit cards.

5 Language
The language of the islands, like the rest of Greece, is modern-day Greek. In its written form, the language uses the Greek alphabet, which has 24 letters from Alpha to Omega. English is also widely spoken here.

6 Telephones
Run by Organismos Tilepikoinonion Ellados (OTE), public telephone booths are available in all towns, hotels and resorts. Prices can vary: local calls are cheap but calls made to nearby towns, islands or other countries can be expensive. Phonecards are available from kiosks.

7 Post Offices
The yellow signs of *tachydromeia*, post offices, are quite distinct and can be found in all major towns and villages. Opening timings are usually 7:30am–2pm. Letter boxes are bright yellow as well.

8 Internet
The islands have good Internet connections, and although not all homes have web access, most businessess do. Hotels offer guests online access and every town will have its share of Internet cafés.

9 Newspapers and Magazines
Major European and British newspapers are generally available in hotels and kiosks the day after they are published, although the price mark-up can be substantial. International magazines are also available, as are locally produced publications in English and Greek, which chiefly advise readers on up-and-coming cultural events in the islands.

10 Television and Radio
Hotels and resorts usually have satellite television with a choice of international news and lifestyle channels. Greece has state-owned television and radio stations, as well as several privately owned stations, that are available in the Ionians. However, the transmission and production quality is mixed.

Useful Numbers
• Directory Enquiries: 11888 • International Directory Enquires: 11889 • Code for domestic calls within Greece: 11889 • To send a telegram: 136 • Time: 14844

Dialling Codes
Greece's country code is +30 followed by the five-digit island code and the five-digit private number. Island Codes:
• Corfu: 26610
• Paxí & Antipaxi: 26620
• Lefkáda: 26450
• Kefalloniá: 26740
• Ithaki: 26740
• Zákynthos: 26950

Left **An ambulance** Right **A police patrol vehicle**

🔟 Security and Health

1 Emergency Numbers

In case of an emergency call 100 for police assistance, 166 for an ambulance and 199 to alert the nearest fire department. The Coast Guard can be called by ship radio or by dialling 108. Response times to emergency calls are generally good throughout the Ionians, although slower in the villages.

🕭 *For non-urgent medical advice in the Ionians:*
• *Corfu: 26610 88223*
• *Paxí: 26620 31466*
• *Lefkáda: 26450 25371*
• *Kefalloniá: 26710 23230*
• *Ithaki: 26740 32222*
• *Zákynthos: 26950 23166*

2 Police

There are two divisions of police in the Ionians, the tourist police *(see p102)*, who monitor restaurants, hotels, resorts and venues catering to tourists, and the regular police service.

3 Ambulance

Medical facilities are good in the major towns, less so in the villages. Call 166 for an ambulance in the event of a medical emergency.

4 Fire

Fire-department vehicles in the Ionians are bright red, and therefore easy to identify. Like residents, visitors should be vigilant and keep a lookout for, and report, fires immediately.

Fires begin with some regularity in the heat of summer throughout the region and can spread rapidly along tinder-dry roadsides.

5 Health Insurance

EU citizens are entitled to free emergency medical care as reciprocal arrangements are in place with Greece and its islands. Before travelling, visitors should obtain a European Health Insurance Card (EHIC), available from the Department of Health. The EHIC does not replace health insurance. Non-EU citizens must have medical insurance.

6 Hospitals

Greek National Health Service facilities on the Ionian islands, especially the smaller ones, can be limited, although larger towns have modern hospitals with accident and emergency departments and English-speaking staff. Air ambulances are available to fly serious emergency cases to the state-of-the-art hospitals in Athens if necessary.

7 Dental Care

Most dentists in the Ionians are trained in the city of Athens or in countries such as the UK. As such, the standard of care and knowledge is high. Dental practices are run on a private basis with fees for emergency

treatment payable immediately. Receipts are given for insurance claims.

8 Pharmacies

Pharmacists are highly trained and can advise on ailments and injuries as well as prescribe and dispense medicines. The range of medication is usually extensive. However, it is advisable to pack an adequate supply of regular medication sufficient for the length of your stay. Pharmacies are easily identified by their distinct green cross.

9 Doctors

Hotels will usually recommend local doctors who can assist with more minor medical problems. Most speak good English. As with dentists, fees are payable immediately on treatment and a receipt given for insurance claims. Serious or emergency medical situations should always be referred to a hospital.

10 Crime

The crime rate in Greece is low, especially in the Ionians. However, visitors should be vigilant at all times and avoid putting themselves or others in dangerous situations. It is wise to take sensible precautions, such as keeping all documents together, using a safe for valuables and locking your car securely *(see p107)*.

Left **A picnic in the countryside** Right **Camping in a forest**

Budget Tips

Low Season
Corfu and the Ionians are year-round destinations if warm summer sunshine is not your main holiday requirement. Winter days can be mild and offer many opportunities to explore, hike or trek in tolerable weather. Holiday packages are often much cheaper during the low season.

Cheap Flights
Explore the possibility of booking a low-cost flight and then accommodation separately. If you can be flexible about departure dates and can book several weeks in advance, you are likely to get the best airfare deals. You can also check with your agent for last-minute deals on flights and accommodation.

Discounts
Travel companies often offer discounts for early bookings, which can amount to some substantial savings. Senior citizens and students are entitled to free admission at many museums and archaeological sites in the Ionians, as well as reduced admission fees at other tourist attractions, as long as they are able to show some valid proof of age.

Self-Catering
For a cost-effective and comfortable stay try self-catering accommodation, which can be lots of fun. Buying groceries from the local market and preparing your own meal, while staying at a self-catering apartment or rural home are just some of the joys of an Ionian holiday.

Hostels
The islands have long been a popular destination for backpackers, and a good selection of hostel-style accommodation has developed from this trend. Although not luxurious and rarely offering a range of facilities, hostels are usually comfortable and can be good places to stay for anyone on a tight budget.

Camping
There are inexpensive camp sites dotted around the islands. Some of these are in fabulous beachside locations, while others are set in forests, or olive groves, or on terraced hills. Showers are available at most sites, and many also have restaurants, supermarkets and, in some cases, leisure facilities, such as swimming pools.

Picnics
All the islands have designated picnic spots, often overlooking picturesque bays or located in beautiful pine forests. Inexpensive and fun to prepare using fresh produce from local markets, picnics may also allow you to mingle with the local people as they are a favourite summer Sunday event for Greek families.

Free Entertainment
Ionian citizens like nothing more than a chance to dance and enjoy folk music, and impromptu festivals take place everywhere in the summer months. Visitors are always welcomed. In August, most villages celebrate harvest festival, while cultural events and open-air concerts are common (see pp52–3).

Working Holidays
EU citizens do not need a work permit in Greece unless they plan to stay longer than 90 days, in which case they must apply for residency. Nationals from other countries, however, need a work permit to seek employment here. Holiday work tends to revolve around tourist areas, so working in a bar or restaurant or driving public vehicles, provided one has the right qualifications, are possibilities.

Hitchhiking
Like the rest of Greece, hitchhiking is acceptable in the islands and motorists tend to be generous in giving lifts. It is a good option for travellers on a budget to get around, and a great way to meet locals. Women travelling alone should exercise caution.

Left **A sign prohibiting photography in a place of worship** Right **Sunbathers on a beach**

TOP 10 Things to Avoid

1 Military Zones

Avoid entering restricted areas marked as military zones for the army, navy or air force, and abstain from taking pictures of any vehicle or building in these zones without express permission. Do not photograph military personnel.

2 Photography

Photography is not permitted inside military zones, churches or monasteries. Always check before taking pictures inside museums, tourist venues, hotels or at archaeological sites. Sometimes photography is allowed, but without the use of flash. The same rules apply to the use of video equipment.

3 Offending your Host

Greek people are extremely sociable and will often extend an invitation to you to dine with their family. Consider this an honour and expect a large gathering. It is polite to take flowers, wine, chocolate or pastries for the host. The norm is to dress in smart casuals unless dining in a top notch restaurant, where formal wear is required.

4 Sunburn

Prolonged sun exposure should be avoided. Always apply plenty of high-factor sun-protection cream, especially if swimming, and wear a hat and good-quality sunglasses. Children and fair-skinned people are particularly vulnerable to sunburn. Heat exhaustion is a serious affliction; take adequate precautions.

5 Dehydration

Always drink plenty of water, even if you are not thirsty, to avoid dehydration. Carry water when visiting archaeological sites and outdoor attractions in particular, as drinking water is not always available in such places. All supermarkets and kiosks stock bottled water. If you do get dehydrated, seek medical help.

6 Mosquitoes

Mosquitoes do not carry serious diseases in Greece, but can leave a nasty bite and transfer germs. If you have a bad reaction to a mosquito bite, a pharmacy should be able to advise on medication. Apply a repellent, especially after dark or when near water, and invest in a plug-in deterrent machine.

7 Scams

It is important to take sensible precautions against becoming the victim of fraud, scams or hard-sell schemes, including property-purchasing deals. Such crime is extremely rare in the Ionians, but there are often unscrupulous people keen to make fast money in any tourist area. Read the small print before signing anything.

8 Crime

Pickpocketing, violent crime, theft from cars and burglaries are rare on the islands, but it is important to be cautious at all times. Take care when carrying your valuables, especially in crowded areas, and be sure to lock your vehicle and accommodation, especially when leaving personal items behind.

9 Drugs

Greek authorities have a zero-tolerance policy when it comes to the use or dealing of drugs, and as a result substance abuse in the islands is exceptionally rare. Carrying drugs into the country will have serious consequences if caught when going through customs. Take a note from your doctor if travelling with prescribed drugs.

10 Dubious Clubs

All major towns have late-night clubs to cater to party-loving visitors, and although the majority of these are good fun, a small proportion are on the unsavoury side. The authorities regularly monitor such venues, making sure they conform to strict codes of conduct, but visitors who prefer a gentler form of evening entertainment would do best to avoid them.

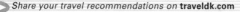

Left **A plate of *souvláki*** Centre **The local spirit, ouzo** Right **A glass of fizzy cola on ice**

🔟 Dining Tips

1 Restaurants
The Ionians offer a fabulous choice of places to eat, but watch out for establishments in tourist areas that advertise international cuisine and have a seemingly endless menu – the chances are the food will be microwaved. That said, there is a good selection of authentic French, Italian, Oriental and even Mexican restaurants to satisfy your tastebuds.

2 Tavernas
A stay in the islands would not be complete without a meal at a traditional taverna. Look out for family-owned establishments that have local dishes on the menu. The meals, such as *kleftiko*, which is meat cooked for hours in a special oven, will almost certainly be freshly prepared and cooked.

3 Cafés and Snack Bars
Cafés, known as *kafeneía*, are an institution throughout Greece and serve as the central point of a community. Every village, however tiny, will have at least one of these cafés serving just coffee with water. However, some now offer sandwiches and light meals, and are more akin to snack bars.

4 Fast Food
All the major Ionian towns have their share of American-style hamburger joints, ice-cream parlours and pizzerias. Local alternatives include *souvlatzídiko* outlets that serve *souvláki*, chunks of pork or chicken chargrilled with herbs. Bakeries have fabulous selections of freshly made pastries.

5 Vegetarians
Greece is a nation of meat-lovers and there are few restaurants catering solely to vegetarians. However, the month-long fast for Lent as part of the Greek Orthodox way of life has ensured that vegetarian recipes have been handed down through generations. These appear on the menus of many tavernas.

6 Local Beers and Spirits
A range of excellent light beers are brewed in Greece, while popular spirits include the aniseed-flavoured ouzo, which turns white when water is added. There are local versions of white rum, brandy and other spirits, while the traditional wine of Greece is retsina. Many villages in the Ionians produce wine.

7 Water
While it is generally safe to drink tap water in the Ionians, it may be wise to buy bottled water from supermarkets or kiosks to avoid the risk of an upset stomach due to unfamiliar chemical content. Alterntively, use boiled water. Hot beverages, such as tea, are usually safe. In restaurants, ensure that you are served bottled water.

8 Soft Drinks
Every town and village will stock a wide range of internationally known soft drinks, plus a selection of locally produced alternatives in bottles and cartons. Fruit juices can be purchased in large cartons and smaller individual packs from supermarkets and kiosks. Restaurants and bars will have a soft-drink selection as well.

9 Menus
Menus at most cafés and restaurants are written in both Greek and English, although in small village tavernas these may be in Greek only. Often diners are invited into the kitchen to choose their meal or are advised as to what is being cooked that day. Check and agree on the price before ordering.

10 Service Charges
A service charge is added to the price of meals on the menu, but this should be clearly stated. Having said that, waiters normally expect extra tips. If the service has been good then consider about 10 per cent of the bill, or a little more if your experience was especially good.

A great way to sample local dishes is to order a meze.

Left **Holiday apartments** Centre **Hotel accreditation sign** Right **Rural villas**

Accommodation Tips

1 High and Low Season

Most hotels have two sets of rates, one for the high season, from June to September, and another for the low season, which runs from October to May. The exceptions are the holiday seasons around Easter, New Year and Christmas, when prices usually rise.

2 Package Holidays

A large number of visitors arrive at the islands on package holidays. Including flights, accommodation, transfers to and from the airport and sometimes car hire and even child care, a package can be a convenient and cost-effective way to plan a great holiday, especially for families.

3 Reservations

It is becoming easier to make reservations with hotels and resorts via the Internet, although the traditional way of making a booking by telephone and fax is still the norm. A credit card may be used to make a deposit, and confirmation is likely to be sent by email or post.

4 Booking Before You Go

It is advisable to book in advance, especially if you wish to stay at a particular location or have specific requirements. Hotels, resorts and villas may be booked many months – even years – in advance by the big tour operators. Booking ahead will also give you peace of mind.

5 Booking When You Get There

Some visitors may prefer the flexibility of arriving and then selecting suitable accommodation. The tourist information office at the airports and in the major towns will have a list of available hotels, resorts and villas and should assist you in your search for a suitable place to stay.

6 Tipping

It is not generally necessary to tip if a hotel employee has shown you to your room, although if the person has been particularly helpful or you are staying in a 5-star hotel with porters, then a tip of a few euros is appropriate. You may also consider giving your chamber staff a few euros if the service has been especially good.

7 Hotel Grading

The Greek National Tourist Office is the official body responsible for maintaining the standard of accommodation offered to visitors. Its guidelines are strict, with particular emphasis on the services and facilities a hotel, villa or resort offers. These are regularly monitored.

Grades range from A down to E, and an L grade is awarded to high-end luxury hotels.

8 Apartments

Whether in a resort, urban complex or a village establishment, apartments designated for tourists come under the same Greek National Tourist Office's classification system. The grade and the price is dependent on the facilities offered, such as swimming pools, a children's playground, maid service, the number of bedrooms and cooking provision.

9 Villas

Located close to towns or in the depths of the countryside, villas usually have from two to four bedrooms, although some are even larger. Before hiring a villa, check if it is fully equipped. Most provide a swimming pool with sun loungers, while others may offer a spa tub as well.

10 Rural Properties

Staying in a private rural villa or in the village home of a local offers the opportunity to really get away from it all and sample a traditional way of life first hand. Villas are often privately advertised or booked via a specialist company, while villagers often rent out spare rooms, which can be found simply by asking at the local coffee shop.

Check **www.greekislandsclub.com** for apartment and villa rentals in the Ionians.

Left **Bella Venezia** Right **Paxós Beach Hotel**

Luxury and Mid-Range Hotels

1 Divani Corfu Palace

This luxury hotel is surrounded by olive groves and overlooks the sea. It has well-equipped guest rooms, swimming pools, a spa and fitness suite. ✆ Map D4 • Kanóni, Corfu Town, Corfu • 26610 38996 • Disabled Access • www.divanis.com • €€€€€

2 Marbella Corfu

The 5-star eco-friendly Marbella Corfu exudes understated luxury. The guestrooms here are exquisite, and on-site facilities include a spa, fitness centre, swimming pool, concert hall and restaurants. ✆ Map D5 • Agios Ioannis, Corfu • 26610 71183 • Disabled Access • www.marbella.gr • €€€€

3 Pelecas Country Club

This luxurious retreat has a beautifully restored mansion, charming out-buildings, a summer-house and stables, many of which date from the 18th century. ✆ Map C4 • Pélekas, Corfu • 26610 52239 • www.country-club.gr • €€€€€

4 Grecotel Corfu Imperial

Sitting enticingly on a private peninsula overlooking the bay of Corfu, this charming 5-star hotel offers fabulous sea-view rooms, an Italianate garden and private coves to explore. Facilities include gourmet restaurants and berthing for yachts. ✆ Map C3 • Kommeno, Corfu • 26610 88400 • Disabled Access • www.grecotel.com • €€€€€

5 Corfu Palace

Recognized around the world as one of Corfu's top hotels, this luxurious palace stands in lush gardens overlooking Garitsa bay. Its 115 beautifully appointed rooms and suites include facilities such as a marble bath. A spa is also on site. ✆ Map P2 • Leoforos Dimokratias 2, Corfu Town, Corfu • 26610 39485 • Disabled Access • www.corfupalace.com • €€€€€

6 Gelina Village

This luxurious hotel and resort of apartments has a spa, water park, history museum and sports centre. The hotel's decorative and architectural theme is a mixture of Classical, Byzantine and Corfiot. The restaurant here is particularly good, and uses local produce only. ✆ Map C1 • Acharávi, Corfu • 26630 64000 • Disabled Access • www.gelinavillage.gr • €€€€

7 Iberostar Kerkyra Golf

A family-orientated resort, this 4-star beachside complex offers a mini club for children, playground and pools. As the name suggests, it is popular with golf enthusiasts; it is a short drive from an 18-hole golf course. Guests can also enjoy its tennis courts, indoor and outdoor restaurants and shops, or stroll in its Mediterranean-style gardens. ✆ Map E5 • Alykés Potámou, Corfu • 26610 24030 • www.louishotels.com • €€€

8 Bella Venezia

This elegant hotel is a glorious apricot-washed Neo-Classical mansion that was once the home of one of Corfu's foremost families. It offers 31 exquisite rooms and a bar reminiscent of an English pub. ✆ Map P2 • Corfu Town, Corfu • 26610 46500 • Disabled Access • www.bellaveneziahotel.com • €€€

9 Cavalieri Hotel

Recently refurbished in an elegant country-house style, this hotel was once home to a 17th-century nobleman. It has panoramic sea views and offers well-equipped guest rooms. Evening drinks are served at the roof-top garden here. ✆ Map Q6 • 4 Kapodistriou, Corfu Town, Corfu • 26610 39041 • www.cavalieri-hotel.com • €€€

10 Paxós Beach Hotel

Beautifully presented in local stone, this waterfront hotel overlooks one of Paxí's prettiest bays. Its terrace-restaurant offers panoramic views of the bay. ✆ Map B5 • Gáios, Paxí • 26620 32211 • www.paxosbeachhotel.gr • €€€

An increasing number of hotels now provide facilities and access for people with disabilities.

Price Categories

For a standard, double room per night (with breakfast if included), taxes and extra charges.

€	under €50
€€	€50–100
€€€	€100–200
€€€€	€200–300
€€€€€	over €300

Above **Pink Palace**

🔟 Budget Stays and Camp Sites

1 Fundana Hotel
Set in gardens of bougainvillea and almond trees, this hotel is a restored 17th-century Venetian mansion. Little courtyards give it an intimate character. It has a swimming pool, and the guest rooms and studios are chic and inviting. ⊗ *Map B3 • 1 Odysseos, Paleokastrítsa, Corfu • 26630 22532 • www. fundanavillas.com • €€*

2 Casa Lucia
Set in the countryside near the coast, this cottage-complex offers an escape from the fast lane. It comprises former olive-press buildings that have been converted into individual bungalows. On-site yoga and t'ai chi lessons are available. ⊗ *Map C3 • Sgombou, Corfu • 26610 91419 • www.casa-lucia-corfu.com • €€*

3 Pink Palace
Living up to its name, this sprawling pink-washed hotel-cum-hostel is great value for money. It is set on a private beach and boasts a roof-garden restaurant and nightclub. Several sport-based activities are on offer here. ⊗ *Map C4 • Agios Gordios Beach, Sinarades, Corfu • 26610 53103 • www.thepink palace.com • €*

4 Anemona Studios
Lying on the edge of the Paleokastrítsa resort, these well-equipped studios promise peace and quiet. Some of its ten apartments have private balconies. Guests may use the swimming pool of the Phivos Studios nearby. ⊗ *Map B3 • Paleokastrítsa, Corfu • 26630 41101 • www. paleo kastritsaholidays.com • €*

5 Hotel Bretagne
Located within easy reach of Corfu Town's attractions, this recently renovated hotel is slick and stylish. Its inside and alfresco restaurants and bar are charming, while its well-equipped guest rooms have a pleasing home-from-home feel. ⊗ *Map N3 • 27 K. Georgaki, Corfu Town, Corfu • 26610 30724 • www.corfuhotel bretagne.com • €€*

6 Hotel Avrilios
Situated in the small town of Lefkimmi, this charming 2-star apartment hotel offers value for money. Its apartments are well appointed, while the main complex has a restaurant and swimming pool. ⊗ *Map E6 • Lefkimmi, Corfu • 26610 61262 • €*

7 Dionysus Camping Village
Providing a choice of tents, bungalows and shady places in which to shelter caravans and motor homes, this is one of the oldest and most popular camp sites on Corfu. Amenities include shower blocks, laundry, supermarket and restaurant. ⊗ *Map C3 • Darnilas Bay, Dasía, Corfu • 26610 91417 • www. dionysuscamping.gr • €*

8 Paleokastrítsa Camping
Set in the heart of the countryside, this camp site offers conveniences such as shower blocks, electricity and a children's play area. Caravans, camper vans and visitors keen to sleep under canvas are welcome here. ⊗ *Map B3 • Paleokastrítsa, Corfu • 26630 41101 • www.paleokastritsa holidays.com • €*

9 Hotel Zafiris
With views out over the Canal d'Armour, this collection of rooms and studios, set around gardens and walkways, is a popular 2-star option. Its Waterfalls Restaurant uses fresh produce from the hotel's own organic gardens. ⊗ *Map A1 • Melitsa, Perouládes, Corfu • 26630 99321 • www.zafiris-corfu.gr • €*

10 Clara Studios
Located next to the Folk Museum and ideal for enjoying Paxí's lively capital, Gäios, this traditional white-washed studio complex is beautifully presented. Many of the studios have balconies with great views over the town and are equipped with all necessities for a comfortable stay. ⊗ *Map B5 • Gäios, Paxí • 26620 32313 • €*

Note: Unless otherwise stated, all hotels accept credit cards and have en-suite bathrooms.

Left **The Ionian Blue's Scorpios lounge bar** Right **Interior of the Alexandros Hotel**

Luxury and Mid-Range Hotels

1 Ionian Blue
Built on a hillside with panoramic views out over the sea, this is one of Lefkáda's leading luxury hotels. Amenities include a spa, beauty suite, pools, a gym, restaurants and a lounge bar. ◈ Map J2 • Nikiana, Lefkáda • 26450 29029 • Disabled Access • www. ionianblue.gr • €€€€€

2 Armonia
Built in traditional Greek style, complete with roof timbers and terraces, this attractive hotel overlooks the stunning coastline of Nydrí and its adjacent islands. Guest rooms are well furnished, and amenities include a cocktail bar. ◈ Map J2 • Megalo Avlaki, Nydrí, Lefkáda • 26450 92751 • www.hotel-armonia-lefkada.gr • €€€€

3 Grand Nefeli Hotel
Standing in gardens that hug the beach, this apricot-washed hotel is a prominent complex on the coast at Vasilikí, a paradise for windsurfers. It has its own windsurfing tutors for those keen to give the sport a try. ◈ Map H2 • Ponti, Vasilikí, Lefkáda • 26450 31378 • Disabled Access • www. grandnefeli.com • €€€€

4 Neion Hotel
This hotel, with its traditional Greek architectural features, such as open fireplaces and wooden window shutters, comprises three stone buildings, which have been beautifully restored. Located in the pretty village of Kiafa, it boasts a dining terrace that looks out over a rural landscape. ◈ Map J2 • Kiafa, Alexandros, Lefkáda • 26450 41624 • www.neion.gr • €€€

5 Porto Galini Hotel
This delightful hotel is made up of several small traditionally styled buildings linked by walkways. It has sports facilities and a spa, along with well-presented guest rooms. The hotel welcomes children. ◈ Map J2 • Maggana, Nikiana, Lefkáda • 26450 92433 • www.portogalini. gr • €€€€

6 Portofico Hotel
This family-run hotel is located beside the beautiful Ponti beach and offers 29 charming guest rooms and a stylish restaurant dotted around a swimming pool and children's pool. All rooms have balconies and good facilities. ◈ Map H2 • Ponti, Vasilikí, Lefkáda • 26450 31402 • www. portoficohotel.gr • €€€

7 Alexandros Hotel
Set in extensive beachside gardens, this fabulously chic hotel is one of Nikiana's finest. As well as stylish guest rooms, it offers leisure and fitness amenities, children's play areas and a large conference centre that caters to its business clientele. ◈ Map J2 • Nikiana, Lefkáda • 26450 71120 • www.hotel alexandros.com • €€€€

8 Agios Nikitas
This hotel has been built in a traditional Greek style. It is close to the beach and its proximity to the village offers visitors the chance to experience local culture. Be sure to go for breakfast here – it is served in a pretty flagstone courtyard. ◈ Map J2 • Nikiana, Lefkáda • 26450 97460 • www.agiosnikitas.gr • €€€

9 Apóllon Hotel
Nestling on a hillside on Vasilikí's outskirts, this pleasant hotel offers 40 good-size guest rooms with panoramic views of the harbour, the countryside and the sea. A roof terrace provides the perfect place for relaxation. ◈ Map H2 • Vasilikí, Lefkáda • 26450 31122 • Disabled Access • €€

10 Captain Stavros
Located in Lefkáda's lively town of Nydrí, the elegant new Captain Stavros is the epitome of sophistication. The hotel building was designed to resemble a ship, and the interiors are plush. There is also an attractive swimming pool and terrace area. ◈ Map J2 • Nydrí, Lefkáda • 26450 93333 • www.captain stavros-hotel.gr • €€€€€

Price Categories

For a standard, double room per night (with breakfast if included), taxes and extra charges.

€	under €50
€€	€50–100
€€€	€100–200
€€€€	€200–300
€€€€€	over €300

Left **St George's House**

🔟 Budget Stays and Camp Sites

1 Ostria Hotel
Sitting high above Agios Nikitas, one of the prettiest coastal villages on the island, this small *pension*-style hotel has 12 guest rooms, a restaurant and a bar decorated in traditional Greek style. 🗺 *Map H1 • Agios Nikitas, Lefkáda • 26450 97483 • €*

2 Arion Hotel
The Arion comprises 12 attractively furnished studios and apartments, and has warm and helpful staff. Although it has few amenities, its location in central Perigiali ensures traditional tavernas are never far away. It is around 300 m (1,000 ft) from the beach. 🗺 *Map J2 • Perigiali, Lefkáda • 26450 92257 • €*

3 Bel Air Hotel
Set in the heart of Nydrí and offering facilities such as swimming and spa pools, a children's pool, bars and a dining terrace, Bel Air offers great value for money. The hotel's 33 air-conditioned apartments have been recently refurbished. 🗺 *Map J2 • Nydrí, Lefkáda • 26450 92125 • www. hotel-belair.gr • €€*

4 Póros Beach Camping
Looking out over the award-winning Póros beach on Lefkáda's southeastern point, this modern camp site offers individual studios and an area for around 70 tents.

On site is a restaurant, laundry, Internet connection and leisure amenities. 🗺 *Map J2 • Mykros Gialos, Lefkáda • 26450 95452 • Disabled Access • www. porosbeach.com.gr • €*

5 Eva Beach Hotel
This small but pretty beachside hotel is ideal for family holidays. Among the amenities for children are high chairs, baby cots, a play area and pool. The hotel is within walking distance of the resort's shops. 🗺 *Map J2 • Nydrí, Lefkáda • 26450 92545 • www.evabeach.gr • €€*

6 St George's House
Located high on a hill overlooking the sea, this small hotel is a great budget option. The rooms are beautifully designed, and the well-kept gardens comprise a swimming pool, attractive terraces and borders bursting with Mediterranean shrubs. 🗺 *Map J1 • Lygia, Lefkáda • 26450 71114 • www. stgeorgeshouse.gr • €€*

7 Vliho Bay
The decor in this hotel, which is set in a pretty bay just south of Nydrí on the east coast of the island, echoes the traditional Greek blue-and-white theme. Most of its air-conditioned guest rooms are located around its swimming pool area. 🗺 *Map J2 • Geni, Ormos Vlychos, Lefkáda 26450 95619 • www.vlihobay.com • €€*

8 Vyzantion Village
A hotel-village complex that welcomes animals, Vyzantion is a great place to stay if you are travelling with your pet. The complex lies in the heart of Lefkáda Town, not far from the Market Square and the pretty area by the harbour. 🗺 *Map J1 • Delpherd, Lefkáda Town, Lefkáda • 26450 22629 • €*

9 Vasilikí Beach Camping
Superbly located in a scenic rural landscape only a short walk from the beach at Vasilikí, this camping complex is a great place to unwind and relax. Although offering few modern amenities, the camp site is well organized and close to the attractions of the southern region of Lefkáda. 🗺 *Map H3 • Ormos Vasilikís, Lefkáda • 26450 31308 • Disabled Access • €*

10 Adani Hotel
Comprising a collection of pleasingly presented guest rooms, this small hotel is in the traditional village of Tsoukalades, a little way from central Lefkáda Town. The hotel offers several amenities, including a children's playground and swimming pool, and is conveniently located to the beach. 🗺 *Map H1 • Tsoukalades, Lefkáda • 26450 97450 • www.adani.gr • €€*

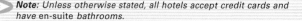

Note: *Unless otherwise stated, all hotels accept credit cards and have en-suite bathrooms.*

Left **Swimming pool at Kefalloniá Grace Emelisse Hotel** Right **Ionian Plaza Hotel**

🔟 Luxury and Mid-Range Hotels

1 Apostolata Hotel
Situated on a hillside gently sloping down to the sea, this beautiful hotel is one of the island's finest. It is a short distance from Skála village. Among its features are a spa and the Sea Pearl and Sunrise restaurants. ⊛ Map J6 • Skála, Kefalloniá • 26710 83581 • Disabled Access • www.louishotels.com • €€€€

2 Cefalonia Garden Village
Offering all-inclusive packages, this complex of nearly 300 apartments lies beside the beach at Agios Giannis. Facilities include a pool with seven water slides for children. ⊛ Map G5 • Agios Giannis beach, Lixoúri, Kefalloniá • 26710 94403 • Disabled Access • €€€

3 Cephalonia Palace
This modern 4-star hotel lies between the deep-red sandy Xi beach and the main thoroughfare in the town centre. It offers a freshwater swimming pool, children's pool and a range of activities, from water sports to bowling. ⊛ Map G6 • Xi Lixoúriou, Kefalloniá • 26710 92555 • www.kefaloniapalacehotel.gr • €€€€

4 Kefalloniá Grace Emelisse Hotel
Guests can enjoy luxury and seclusion at this chic top-end boutique hotel. Surrounded by cypress trees and located on the seashore, this hotel has everything from gourmet restaurants to an infinity pool. ⊛ Map H3 • Emplysi bay, Fiskárdo, Kefalloniá • 26740 41200 • www.arthotel.gr • €€€€€

5 Erissos Palace Hotel
Housed in a traditional and beautifully presented building with a courtyard garden, this attractive hotel, although small, is one of the best in town. It lies in Maganos village, near St Jerusalem beach and Fiskárdo. ⊛ Map H4 • Maganos, Kefalloniá • 26740 41350 • www.erissospalace.gr • €€€

6 Méditerranée Hotel
This hotel organizes sports, children's events and special Greek evenings for those who wish to hear traditional music and sample local fare. The view of the Lixoúri peninsula from the dining terrace is outstanding. ⊛ Map G6 • Lássi, Kefalloniá • 26710 28760 • Disabled Access • www.mediterranee-kefalonia.com • €€€€

7 Ionian Plaza Hotel
This landmark hotel, set in a Neo-Classical building, stands in the centre of Argostóli. It overlooks a palm tree-studded plaza, which becomes a hive of activity in the evening, when people dine alfresco-style here. The Ionian Plaza has a plush and contemporary interior with well-appointed rooms. ⊛ Map G5 • Vallianou Square, Argostóli, Kefalloniá • 26710 25581 • www.ionianplaza.gr • €€€

8 Porto Skála Hotel Village
Designed to resemble a traditional Greek village, the brightly coloured studios here are positioned so all have a sea view. Swimming pools, a gym, Greek events and parties are just some of the draws. ⊛ Map J6 • Agios Georgios, Skála, Kefalloniá • 26710 83501 • www.portoskala.com • €€€

9 White Rocks
Named after the necklace of white rocks and beaches that characterize this stretch of coastline, White Rocks is a 4-star resort that specializes in home-made dishes cooked in its traditional oven hut. ⊛ Map G6 • Platýs Yalos, Kefalloniá • 26710 28332 • www.whiterocks.gr • €€€

10 Faros Suites
This complex of luxury self-catering suites lies in the unspoilt coastal town of Fiskárdo. Each suite is decorated in a Classical style, from the alabaster lamps to the period furniture, and sits close to the swimming pool and garden terraces. ⊛ Map H4 • Fiskárdo, Kefalloniá • 26740 41355 • www.farossuites.gr • €€€

If you plan to visit between November and March, it is advisable to book your hotel ahead as many close during this time.

Price Categories

For a standard, double room per night (with breakfast if included), taxes and extra charges.

€	under €70
€€	€70–100
€€€	€100–150
€€€€	€150–200
€€€€€	over €200

Above **Reception area at the Olga Hotel**

🔟 Budget Stays and Camp Sites

1 Odyssey Apartments
This complex is a real gem, with many well-equipped studios and apartments, some of which have balconies with fabulous views out over the harbourside. It is situated a short distance from the beach in Vathý, the capital of Itháki. ✆ *Map J4 • Vathý, Ithaki • 26740 33400 • www.ithaki-odyssey.com • €€*

2 Alegro Hotel
Famous for fabulous sea views from its isolated perch at the foot of the St George fortress, this 2-star hotel is ideal for a relaxing, affordable holiday. It lies on the town's outskirts, but is close to local restaurants. ✆ *Map G5 • Avenue Hoida, Argostóli, Kefalloniá • 26710 22268 • €€*

3 Linardos Hotel
Sitting near a picturesque bay in Asos, this charming collection of studios and two-storey apartments, most with views out over the bay, is nicely presented and has friendly staff. Facilities include a mini-fridge, television and a daily maid service. ✆ *Map H4 • Asos, Kefalloniá • 26740 51563 • www.linardos apartments.gr • €€*

4 Olga Hotel
Located beside a palm tree-studded quayside, this pretty Venetian-style hotel has 42 modern guest rooms. Facilities include a fridge and air conditioning in rooms, and a charming breakfast lounge overlooking the water. ✆ *Map G5 • Paralia Antoni Tritsi 82, Argostóli, Kefalloniá • 26710 24981 • www.olgahotel.gr • €€*

5 Galini Hotel
Located in Póros, this popular hotel is close to local amenities. Although small and only partially air conditioned, each of its ten guest rooms are well appointed and have a balcony. The hotel offers great views out over the Ionian Sea from most of the rooms. ✆ *Map J6 • Laghia, Póros, Kefalloniá • 26740 72353 • €*

6 Riviera Hotel
Although offering few amenities, this 1-star hotel is spendidly located overlooking the Ionian Sea and the surrounding countryside of Póros. Its rooms are basic but comfortable, its well-lit restaurant serves local cuisine and its staff are helpful and friendly. ✆ *Map J6 • Póros, Kefalloniá • 26740 72327 • €*

7 Póros House Hotel
A traditionally styled collection of apartments, each of which is equipped with a fridge and television, Póros House Hotel is located in Póros town to the north of Skála. For guests on a budget who require a central place to stay, this 13-room complex is an ideal option. ✆ *Map J6 • Póros, Kefalloniá • 26740 72417 • €€*

8 Argostóli Camp Site
Located amongst olive and almond trees, and just minutes on foot from the nearest beach at Argostóli's lighthouse end, this pleasant camp site has wooden huts and space for over 150 tents. Communal facilities include barbecues and a music hall with entertainment. ✆ *Map G5 • Argostóli, Kefalloniá • 26710 23487 • www. argostolibeach.gr • €*

9 Anassa Hotel
The 2-star Anassa Hotel is a popular and inexpensive option in Skála. Located right beside a sandy beach, the hotel has modern interiors, well-equipped guest rooms and amenities such as a pool and barbecue area. ✆ *Map J6 • Skála, Kefalloniá • 26710 83070 • Disabled Access • www.anassahotel.gr • €€€*

10 Grivas Gerasimos Apartments
A short walk from Vathý harbour and with views out over the bay, these two- and three-bedroom apartments provide a convenient base. Facilities include air conditioning, a well-equipped kitchen and daily maid service. ✆ *Map J4 • Vathý Bay, Ithaki • 26740 33328 • €€*

Note: Unless otherwise stated, all hotels accept credit cards and have en-suite bathrooms.

Left **Astir Palace** Right **Pool-side lounge of Caravel Zante**

🔟 Luxury and Mid-Range Hotels

Mabely Grand
One of the finest hotels on Zákynthos, the Mabely Grand in the resort of Kambi has an understated elegance. Guests can enjoy meals on the restaurant terrace overlooking the Ionian Sea or try local dishes in Byzantine, the traditional Greek taverna. ⓢ Map M2 • Kambi, Zákynthos • 26950 41302 • Disabled Access • www.mabely.gr • €€€€€

Mediterranean Beach Resort
Located on the beach at Laganás, this large, modern hotel offers everything needed for a lively holiday, with pools, an Internet connection and leisure facilities that include a gym. ⓢ Map L3 • Laganás, Zákynthos • 26950 55230 • Disabled Access • www.medbeach.gr • €€€€€

Hotel Palatino
One of Zákynthos Town's best hotels, this 4-star establishment has well-decorated rooms and its own café, the Palatino Café, and a cocktail bar. It lies just 100 m (300 ft) from the seafront. ⓢ Map L4 • Kolokotroni St 10, Zákynthos Town, Zákynthos • 26950 27780 • Disabled Access • www.palatinohotel.gr • €€€€

Astir Palace
One of the most attractive resort-style hotels along the Laganás beach strip, this hotel is fresh, modern and welcoming. It has 120 rooms with balconies that overlook the sea, plus restaurants, a swimming pool and air conditioning. ⓢ Map L3 • Laganás, Zákynthos • 26950 53300 • Disabled Access • www.astirhotels.gr • €€€€

Caravel Zante
The 165 guest rooms of this Tsiliví resort are beautifully presented, with sea views from most balconies. A fun park on site makes it ideal for families. Facilities include restaurants and a theatre. ⓢ Map L3 • Plános, Tsiliví, Zákynthos • 26950 45261 • Disabled Access • www.caravelzante.gr • €€€€

Diana Palace
This cosmopolitan hotel lying just outside Zákynthos Town, beside the beach at Argasí, promises a refreshing stay. With 140 well-presented guest rooms, it offers a wide range of facilities, including mini golf, a gym and a children's playground. ⓢ Map M2 • Argasí, Zákynthos • 26950 23070 • Disabled Access • www.dianahotels.gr • €€€

Ilaria Hotel
A spacious poolside area, complete with an ornamental bridge and lavish gardens, offers a backdrop to the attractive, traditionally styled 4-star Ilaria Hotel. Amenities include a children's playground and pools. ⓢ Map M3 • Kalamáki, Zákynthos • 26950 52671 • Disabled Access • www.ilaria.gr • €€€

Katerina Palace Hotel
Conveniently positioned near the sea and close to Zákynthos Town, this hotel offers 105 well-equipped rooms designed with families in mind. All rooms afford views of the sea or the countryside. Greek-themed evenings are a speciality. ⓢ Map M2 • Argasí, Zákynthos • 26950 26998 • www.katerinapalace.com • €€€

Louis Plagos Beach
This sophisticated hotel sits next to the serene Amboula beach, within gardens of palm trees and bougainvillea. It was recently refurbished to a high standard and offers lovely guest rooms, restaurants and new leisure facilities. ⓢ Map L2 • Amboula beach, Zákynthos • 26950 62800 • www.louishotels.com • €€€

Phoenix Beach Hotel
This hotel stands right on Tsiliví's most popular stretch of beach. Rooms are individually designed and the reception and restaurant areas are lavishly presented. ⓢ Map L2 • Tsiliví beach, Zákynthos • 26950 22483 • Disabled Access • www.phoenixbeachhotel.gr • €€€

Most hotels serve a buffet-style breakfast with a good choice of delicious local pastries.

Price Categories

For a standard, double room per night (with breakfast if included), taxes and extra charges.

€ under €50
€€ €50–100
€€€ €100–200
€€€€ €200–300
€€€€€ over €300

Above **A room in the Albatros Apartment Hotel**

🔟 Budget Stays and Camp Sites

1 Leedas Village
This enchanting complex of self-catering stone villas lies near the beach at Lithakia. The interiors radiate character, while outside there are private gardens and communal facilities, such as a barbecue, children's play area and pool. ✆ *Map L3 • Lithakia, Zákynthos • 26950 51305 • www.leedas-village.com • €€*

2 Albatros Apartment Hotel
Comprising 35 tastefully furnished apartments, this hotel is a characterful venue near the beach on the outskirts of the bustling Laganás. Its Albatros Restaurant serves freshly prepared local dishes. ✆ *Map L3 • Laganás, Zákynthos • 26950 51139 • www.albatroshotel.gr • €€*

3 Asteria Hotel
One of the first hotels built in Alykés village, the Asteria is set beside a long sandy beach and has terraces affording panoramic views across the bay. Guest rooms are tastefully presented and amenities here include the Asteria Taverna, a bar and water sports. ✆ *Map L2 • Alykés bay, Zákynthos • 26950 84059 • Disabled Access • €€*

4 Divina Hotel
A collection of furnished apartments, this 2-star hotel has a swimming pool with a special children's play area. It is surrounded by gardens full of Mediterranean shrubs and is located close to the beach and many local amenities. ✆ *Map L3 • Laganás, Zákynthos • 26950 42274 • €*

5 Natali Hotel
Located next to Laganás beach, this hotel is family-orientated, with a children's play area, baby-sitting services, organized outdoor games, swimming pools and air conditioning. Always bustling, it lies near the resort's major attractions. ✆ *Map L3 • Laganás, Zákynthos • 26950 52394 • Disabled Access • €*

6 Sirocco Hotel
This small, attractive white-washed hotel in the village of Kalamáki, has been recently renovated to a good standard. It has tasteful air-conditioned guest rooms and apartments, while its restaurant serves food prepared from traditional recipes. ✆ *Map M3 • Kalamáki, Zákynthos • 26950 26083 • www.siroccohotel.gr • €€*

7 Hotel Alba
A good-value hotel in the heart of Zákynthos Town, the Alba has 15 charming rooms with all the basic amenities. Although there is no on-site restaurant (there is only a lounge and bar), the hotel's staff are always helpful when it comes to choosing a nearby place to dine. ✆ *Map M4 • Labrou Ziva St, Zákynthos Town, Zákynthos • 26950 26641 • www.albahotel.gr • €€*

8 Alykés Camping
Located to the island's northeast, this popular camp site occupies a secluded terrace that extends towards Alykés beach. A shower block, laundry and supermarket are among the facilities here. Apartments are available as well. ✆ *Map L2 • Alykés bay, Zákynthos • 26950 83233 • www.alykescamping.gr • €*

9 Tartaruga Camping
This lively camp site has been a popular place to camp for around 20 years. Highlights include the adjacent beach and a taverna, and there is also a supermarket here. ✆ *Map L3 • Laganás, Zákynthos • 26950 51967 • Disabled Access • www.tartaruga-camping.com • €*

10 Panorama Studio Apartments
Built with traditional balconies and verandas, this complex has 35 great apartments. Its communal swimming pool and sun terraces are a few minutes' walk from Alykés beach and the restaurants located nearby. ✆ *Map L2 • Alykés bay, Zákynthos • 26950 83685 • www.panorama.alykes.com • €€*

➤ **Note:** Unless otherwise stated, all hotels accept credit cards and have en-suite bathrooms.

General Index

Acknowledgments

The Author

Carole French is an award-winning BBC-trained journalist, based in Cyprus and the UK. Her work has appeared in publications including *ABTA Magazine*, *Homes Overseas* and the *Daily Mail*. She has worked on travel guides for Michelin, Time Out and Thomas Cook, and provided expert consultation on the Greek Islands for television.

Photographer Barry Hayden
Additional Photography Paul Harris, Rupert Horrox, Peter Jousiffe, Rob Reichenfeld, Rough Guides/Michelle Grant, Simon Smith, Clive Streeter
Fact Checker Anthony Clark

At DK INDIA

Managing Editor Aruna Ghose
Editorial Mangers Ankita Awasthi, Sheeba Bhatnagar
Design Manager Kavita Saha
Project Editor Yasmin Rahman
Project Designer Namrata Adhwaryu
Assistant Cartographic Manager Suresh Kumar
Cartographers Jasneet Kaur Arora, Zafar-ul-Islam Khan
Senior Picture Research Coordinator Taiyaba Khatoon
Picture Researcher Shweta Andrews
DTP Coordinator Azeem Siddiqui
Indexer Cyber Media Services Ltd.

At DK LONDON

Publisher Douglas Amrine
List Manager Christine Stroyan
Design Manager Mabel Chan
Senior Editor Sadie Smith
Project Editor Alexandra Farrell
Designer Tracy Smith
Senior Cartographic Editor Casper Morris
DTP Operator Jason Little
Production Controller Louise Daly

Picture Credits

Placement Key- t=top; tc=top centre; tr=top right; tl= top left; cla=centre left above; ca=centre above; cra=centre right above; cl=centre left; c=centre; cr=centre right; clb=centre left below; cb=centre below; crb=centre right below; bl=bottom left; bc=bottom centre; br=bottom right.
Every effort has been made to trace the copyright holders, and we apologize in advance for any unintentional omissions. We would be pleased to insert the appropriate acknowledgments in any subsequent edition of this publication.

Photography Permissions

Dorling Kindersley would like to thank the following for their assistance and kind permission to photograph at their establishments:

Achílleion Palace, Corfu; Albatros Apartment Hotel, Zákynthos; Alexandros Hotel, Lefkáda; Archaeological Museum, Corfu; Archaeological Museum, Lefkáda; Bella Venezia, Corfu; Byzantine Museum, Zákynthos; Caravel Zante, Zákynthos; Diaplasi Bookstore, Corfu; Ecclesiastical Museum, Zákynthos; Emelisse Art Lounge Bar, Kefalloniá; Ionian Plaza Hotel, Kefalloniá; Janis Restaurant, Corfu; Lefkáda Beach Restaurant, Lefkáda; Museum of

Asiatic Art, Corfu; Olga Hotel, Kefalloniá; Olive Wood Shop, Corfu; Patsouras Taverna, Kefalloniá; Phonograph Museum, Lefkáda; Sto Mólos, Lefkáda; Taverna Sebastian, Corfu; Taverna Vassilis, Paxí; The Pines Restaurant, Kefalloniá; Tom's Seaside Restaurant, Lefkáda; Veto Bar, Kefalloniá

The publisher would like to thank the following individuals, companies, and picture libraries for their kind permission to reproduce their photographs:

4CORNERS IMAGES: SIME/ Giovanni Simeone 28-29

ALAMY: Classic Image 30tr; Greg Balfour Evans 100-101, 107tr; John Henshall 26cla; James Davis Photography 4-5; Dimitris K. 43tr; Lordprice Collection 30tl; Marka / Giulio Andreini 52tl; Mary Evans Picture Library 36ca; Chris McLennan 63tl; Jeff Morgan 97tl; Brian North 47cl; NRT-Travel 52tr; PCL 63tr; Nicholas Pitt 7cb; Robert Harding Picture Library Ltd 34b,/ Fraser Hall 56tr,/ R H Productions 41cl; Terry Harris just Greece photo library 52br, 106tl; Travel and Places 12-13c

The BRIDGEMAN ART LIBRARY: *Sappho and Phaon*, 1809 (oil on canvas), David, Jacques Louis (1748-1825) / Hermitage, St. Petersburg, Russia 36br.

CORBIS: Bettmann 31cl, 36tl

DR. HARRY GOUVAS: 11bc

THE GRANGER COLLECTION, NEW YORK: 30br, 36tr

PHOTOLIBRARY: Index Stock Imagery /Timothy O'Keefe 8-9c; Jon Arnold Travel/ Danielle Gali 76-77; Nordic Photos / Frank Chmura 24-25c; Robert Harding Travel/ Ellen Rooney 1c; White/ Paolo Negri 54-55

All other images are © Dorling Kindersley. For further information see *www.dkimages.com*

Phrase Book

In an Emergency

Help!	**Voítheia!**	vo-ee-theea!
Stop!	**Stamatíste!**	sta-ma-tee-steh!
Call a doctor!	**Fonáxte éna giatró!**	fo-nak-steh e-na ya-tro!
Call an ambulance/ police/ fire brigade!	**Kaléste to asthenofóro/ tin astynomía/ tin pyrosvestikí!**	ka-le-steh to as-the-no-fo-ro/ teen a-sti-no-mía/ teen pee-ro-zve-stee-kee!
Where is the nearest telephone/ hospital?	**Poú eínai to plisiéstero tiléfono/ nosokomeío?**	poo ee-ne to plee-see-e-ste-ro tee-le-pho-no/ no-so-ko-mee-o?

Communication Essentials

Yes/No	**Nai/Ochi**	neh/o-chee
Please	**Parakaló**	pa-ra-ka-lo
Thank you	**Efcharistó**	ef-cha-ree-sto
Excuse me	**Me synchoreíte**	me seen-cho-ree-teh
Hello	**Geiá sas**	yeea sas
Goodbye	**Antío**	an-dee-o
Good morning	**Kaliméra**	ka-lee-me-ra
Good night	**Kalinýchta**	ka-lee-neech-ta
Morning	**Proí**	pro-ee
Afternoon	**Apógevma**	a-po-yev-ma
Evening	**Vrádi**	vrath-i
Yesterday	**Chthés**	chthes
Today	**Símera**	see-me-ra
Tomorrow	**Avrio**	av-ree-o
Here	**Edó**	ed-o
There	**Ekeí**	e-kee
What?	**Tí?**	tee?
Why?	**Giatí?**	ya-tee?
Where?	**Poú?**	poo?

Useful Phrases

How are you?	**Tí kááneis?**	tee ka-nees
Very well, thank you.	**Poly kalá, efcharistó.**	po-lee ka-la, ef-cha-ree-sto.
Pleased to meet you.	**Chaíro polý.**	che-ro po-lee.
Where is/are…?	**Poú eínai…?**	poo ee-ne…?
How far is it to…?	**Póso apéchei…?**	po-so a-pe-chee?
Do you speak English?	**Miláte Angliká?**	mee-la-te an-glee-ka?
I don't understand.	**Den katalavaíno.**	then ka-ta-la-ve-no.
Could you speak slowly?	**Miláte lígo pio argá parakaló?**	mee-la-te lee-go pyo ar-ga pa-ra-ka-lo?
I'm sorry.	**Me synchoreíte.**	me seen-cho-ree-teh.

Useful Words

big	**Megálo**	me-ga-lo
small	**Mikró**	mi-kro
hot	**Zestó**	zes-to
cold	**Krýo**	kree-o
good	**Kaló**	ka-lo
bad	**Kakó**	ka-ko
enough	**Arketá**	ar-ke-ta
well	**Kalá**	ka-la
open	**Anoichtá**	a-neech-ta
closed	**Kleistá**	klee-sta
left	**Aristerá**	a-ree-ste-ra
right	**Dexiá**	dek-see-a
near	**Kontá**	kon-da
far	**Makriá**	ma-kree-a
up	**Epáno**	e-pa-no
down	**Káto**	ka-to
early	**Norís**	no-rees
late	**Argá**	ar-ga
toilet	**Oi toualétes**	ee-too-a-le-tes

Shopping

How much does this cost?	**Póso kánei?**	po-so ka-nee?
Do you have…?	**Echete…?**	e-che-teh…?
Do you take credit cards/ travellers' cheques?	**Dechneste pistotikés kártes'/ travellers cheques?**	the-ches-teh pee-sto-tee-kes kar-tes'/ travellers' cheques?
What time do you open/ close?	**Póte anoígete/ kleínete?**	po-teh a-nee-ye-teh/ klee-ne-teh?
Can you ship this overseas?	**Mporeíte na to steílete sto exoterikó?**	bo-ree-teh na to stee-le-teh sto e-xo-te-ree ko?

Sightseeing

tourist information	**O EOT**	o E-OT
archaeological	**archaiologikós**	ar-che-o-lo-yee-kos
art gallery	**I gkalerí**	ee ga-le-ree
beach	**I paralía**	ee pa-ra-lee-a
Byzantine	**vyzantinós**	vee-zan-dee-nos
castle	**To kástro**	to ka-stro
cathedral	**I mitrópoli**	ee mee-tro-po-lee
cave	**To spílaio**	to spee-le-o
church	**I ekklísia**	ee e-klee-see-a
folk art	**laïkí téchni**	la-ee-kee tech-nee
historical	**istorikós**	ees-to-ree-kos
island	**To nisí**	to nee-see
library	**I vivliothíki**	ee veev-lee-o-thee-kee
monastery	**moní**	mo-ni
mountain	**To vounó**	to voo-no
museum	**To mouseío**	to moo-see-o
garden	**O kípos**	o kee-pos
gorge	**To farángi**	to fa-ran-gee
road	**O drómos**	o thro-mos
saint	**ágios/ágioi/ agía/agíes**	a-yee-os/a-yee-ee/a-yee-a/a-yee-es
square	**I plateía**	ee pla-tee-a
closed on public holidays	**kleistó tis argíes**	klee-sto tees aryee-es

Staying in a Hotel

Do you have a vacant room?	**Echete domátia?**	e-che-teh tho-ma-tee-a?
double room with double bed	**Díklino me dipló kreváti**	thee-klee-no meh thee-plo kre-va-tee
twin room	**Díklino me moná krevátia**	thee-klee-no meh mo-na kre-vat-ya
single room	**Monóklino**	mo-no-klee-no
key	**To kleidí**	to klee-dee
I have a reservation.	**Echo kánei krátisi.**	e-cho ka-nee kra-tee-see.

Eating Out

Have you got a table?	**Echete trapézi?**	e-che-te tra-pe-zee?
The bill, please.	**Ton logariazmó parakaló.**	ton lo-gar-yas-mo pa-ra-ka-lo.
I am a vegetarian.	**Eímai chortofágos.**	ee-meh chor-to-fa-gos.
What is fresh today?	**Tí frésko échete símera?**	tee fres-ko e-che-teh see-me-ra?
waiter/waitress	**Kýrie/Garson"/ Kyría**	Kee-ree-eh/Gar-son/Kee-ree-a
menu	**O katálogos**	o ka-ta-lo-gos
cover charge	**To "couvert"**	to koo-ver
wine list	**O katálogos me ta oinopne vmatódi**	o ka-ta-lo-gos meh ta ee-no-pnev-ma-to-thee
glass	**To potíri**	to po-tee-ree
bottle	**To mpoukáli**	to bou-ka-lee
knife	**To machaíri**	to ma-che-ree
fork	**To piroúni**	to pee-roo-nee
spoon	**To koutáli**	to koo-ta-lee
breakfast	**To proïnó**	to pro-ee-no
lunch	**To mesimerianó**	to me-see-mer-ya-no
dinner	**To deípno**	to theep-no
main course	**To kyrios gévma**	to kee-ree-os yev-ma
starter/ first course	**Ta orektiká**	ta o-rek-tee-ka
dessert	**To glykó**	ylee-ko
bar	**To "bar"**	To bar
taverna	**I tavérna**	ee ta-ver-na
café	**To kafeneío**	to ka-fe-nee-o
grill house	**I psistariá**	ee psee-sta-rya
wine shop	**To oinopoleío**	to ee-no-po-lee-o
restaurant	**To estiatório**	to e-stee-a-to-ree-o
ouzeri	**To ouzerí**	to oo-ze-ree
meze shop	**To mezedopoleío**	To me-ze-do-po-lee-o
take away	**To souvlatzídiko**	To soo-vlat-zee-dee-ko
kebabs		
rare	**Eláchista psiméno**	e-lach-ees-ta psee-me-no
medium	**Métria psiméno**	met-ree-a psee-me-no
well done	**Kalopsiméno**	ka-lo-psee-me-no

Basic Food and Drink

coffee	**O Kafés**	o ka-fes
with milk	**ma gála**	me ga-la
black coffee	**skétos**	ske-tos
without sugar	**choris záchari**	cho-rees za-cha-ree
medium sweet	**métrios**	me-tree-os
very sweet	**glyk'ys**	glee-kees
tea	**tsái**	tsa-ee
hot chocolate	**zestí sokoláta**	ze-stee so-ko-la-ta
wine	**krasí**	kra-see
red	**kókkino**	ko-kee-no
white	**lefkó**	lef-ko
rosé	**rozé**	ro-ze
raki	**To rakí**	to ra-kee
ouzo	**To oúzo**	to oo-zo
retsina	**I retsína**	ee ret-see-na
water	**To neró**	to ne-ro
octopus	**To chtapódi**	to chta-po-dee
fish	**To psári**	to psa-ree
cheese	**To tyrí**	to tee-ree

halloumi	**To chaloúmi**	to cha-loo-mee
feta	**I féta**	ee fe-ta
bread	**To psomí**	to pso-mee
bean soup	**I fasoláda**	ee fa-so-la-da
houmous	**To houmous**	to choo-moos
meat kebabs	**O gýros**	o yee-ros
Turkish delight	**To loukoúmi**	to loo-koo-mee
baklava	**O mpaklavás**	o bak-la-vas
kleftiko	**To kléftiko**	to klef-tee-ko

Numbers

1	**éna**	e-na
2	**dýo**	thee-o
3	**tría**	tree-a
4	**téssera**	te-se-ra
5	**pénte**	pen-deh
6	**éxi**	ek-si
7	**eptá**	ep-ta
8	**ochtó**	och-to
9	**ennéa**	e-ne-a
10	**déka**	the-ka
11	**énteka**	en-de-ka
12	**dódeka**	tho-the-ka
13	**dekatría**	de-ka-tree-a
14	**dekatéssera**	the-ka-tes-se-ra
15	**dekapénte**	the-ka-pen-de
16	**dekaéxi**	the-ka-ek-si
17	**dekaeptá**	the-ka-ep-ta
18	**dekaochtó**	the-ka-och-to
19	**dekaennéa**	the-ka-e-ne-a
20	**eíkosi**	ee-ko-see
21	**eikosiéna**	ee-ko-see-e-na
30	**triánta**	tree-an-da
40	**saránta**	sa-ran-da
50	**penínta**	pe-neen-da
60	**exínta**	ek-seen-da
70	**evdomínta**	ev-tho-meen-da
80	**ogdónta**	og-thon-da
90	**enenínta**	e-ne-neen-da
100	**ekató**	e-ka-to
200	**diakósia**	thya-kos-ya
1,000	**chília**	cheel-ya

Time, Days and Dates

one minute	**éna leptó**	e-na lep-to
one hour	**mía óra**	mee-a o-ra
half an hour	**misí óra**	mee-see o-ra
a day	**mía méra**	mee-a me-ra
a week	**mía evdomáda**	mee-a ev-tho-ma-tha
a month	**énas mínas**	e-nas mee-nas
a year	**énas chrónos**	e-nas chro-nos
Monday	**Deftéra**	thef-te-ra
Tuesday	**Tríti**	tree-tee
Wednesday	**Tetárti**	te-tar-tee
Thursday	**Pémpti**	pemp-tee
Friday	**Paraskeví**	pa-ras-ke-vee
Saturday	**Sávvato**	sa-va-to
Sunday	**Kyriakí**	keer-ee-a-kee
January	**Ianouários**	ee-a-noo-a-ree-os
February	**Fevrouários**	fev-roo-a-ree-os
March	**Mártios**	mar-tee-os
April	**Aprílios**	a-pree-lee-os
May	**Máios**	ma-ee-os
June	**Ioúnios**	ee-oo-nee-os
July	**Ioúlios**	ee-oo-lee-os
August	**Avgoustos**	av-goo-stos
September	**Septémvrios**	sep-tem-vree-os
October	**Októvrios**	ok-to-vree-os
November	**Noémvrios**	no-em-vree-os
December	**Dekémvrios**	the-kem-vree-os

Selected Town Index